Little House
in the
Cow Paddock

Little House
in the
Cow Paddock

Written and Illustrated by

Wendy Hamilton

ZealAus Publishing

Little House in the Cow Paddock:
Growing Up in New Zealand

Copyright © 2020 by Wendy Hamilton
Illustrations © 2020 by Wendy Hamilton

www.zealauspublishing.com

All rights reserved. No part of this book may be reproduced or transmitted in any form or by any means without written permission of the author. Some names have been changed to protect the identity of persons.

ISBN: 978-1-925888-59-1 (e)
ISBN: 978-1-925888-60-7 (hc)
ISBN: 978-1-925888-61-4 (sc)

Dedication

For John

Contents

Changes Afoot	1
The New Shower	8
Shovels, Picks and a Concrete floor.	18
A Horse for Free	26
The Trip Home	33
Hidden Treasure.	41
The Frame Goes Up	50
The Stick House in the Cow Paddock	58
Preparations for the Horse Show	66
The Horse Show	70
Contractors and Wind.	76
Budding Entrepreneurs	84
The Stall	89
Mum's Comb and a Bold Decision	97
God, Sells the House	103
We Shift Out to Mount Tiger	109
The Walls Go Up	117
Mum's Curlers	124
The House is Finished	130
About the Author	139
Other Children's Books By Wendy Hamilton	140

Little House in the Cow Paddock

Changes Afoot

Rubella lolled on the lounge floor colouring in while Antoinette painted her fake nails bright red.

"Well, I've done it," said Mum, putting down the phone, "I've listed the house with a land agent."

"I can't wait to live at Mount Tiger all the time, instead of only weekends," I said, thinking of Wuzzel my elderly horse with rickety legs.

"Me too," said Rubella, thinking of Larry her pet sheep.

"I corn't wait to tell the girls at school Dad is building us a new house on our country estate," said Antoinette, speaking in a posh English accent.

Rubella rolled her eyes and I hid a smile. The way Antoinette described our forty-acre hobby-farm in the bush made it seem like the grounds of Buckingham Palace.

"Joanne will be so jealous of my new bedroom,"

said Antoinette blowing on her fingers, "she has to share a dingy room with her little sister."

"Meagan has her own room," said Rubella, colouring the ball on a seal's nose blue. She glanced at Antoinette from the corner of hooded eyes, eager to see if her shot hit home.

"Yes, and it's huge," said Antoinette, dropping back into her normal New Zealand accent. "You can bet my room will be smaller than hers," she added bitterly, "I wish I was an only child like her."

"Does she have a four-poster-bed?" asked Rubella slyly.

"Nooo," said Antoinette brightening (the posh accent was back) "can I have a four-poster-bed, Mum?"

"Don't be silly," said Mum sharply. "What's that on your fingers?" she said, suddenly noticing Antoinette's bright red fingernails.

"Nail polish," said Antoinette lifting up her nose and looking down, "Meagan gave it to me."

"Don't get any of that on the carpet," growled Mum, spotting the bottle of nail polish sitting on the floor, "put the cap back on this instant!"

Antoinette pouted, but did as she was told.

"As I was saying, Harold," said Mum, sinking into an armchair and taking up her knitting, "the land agent is a lovely little man. So quiet hardly said a word, so I let him list it as a sole agency." Her quick finger's looped wool expertly as the needles flashed. "He said this is a nice house in a good area so it shouldn't take

Little House in the Cow Paddock

too long to sell." She pulled at the yarn and the ball of wool rolled towards the honky-tonk piano. Shnike meowed, shot like a black streak from under Mum's chair, and whacked the ball with his paw.

"Maybe?" Dad cleared his throat and intoned heavily, "everything takes ten times longer than you expect."

The rest of the family ignored the familiar statement, but I seized it as a golden opportunity to complain.

"Yes," I agreed, it is taking ten times longer than I expected to get a proper shower at Mount Tiger?"

The subject was an emotive one. As my words flew into the room, I struck the bullseye with Antoinette.

"I would die of mortification if Meagan ever saw our shower," she moaned, pouncing on the cat. She cradled him like a baby and tickled his tummy.

"I don't know why you are worrying about Meagan," I said snippily, jealous that she had the cat. "The chances of your hoity-toity friend popping up in the bush while you are showering is zero. A lost tramper or a busload of Japanese tourists is much more likely," I added sourly. "What's more they carry cameras."

"Oh, for Pete's sake, Wendy, don't be so dramatic," said Mum impatiently, "all this talk of Japanese tourists is silly. Besides, the tea-tree and the ferns are so thick it's perfectly private."

I scowled and held my peace, but I noticed Mum said nothing about the trampers which confirmed my fears.

Wendy Hamilton

"When are we going to get a better shower?"

Little House in the Cow Paddock

"I'm going to take a photo of our shower and send it to Meagan," smirked Rubella, starting on another picture. "I bet she will get a surprise when she sees it's a yellow watering-can hanging off a big old tree."

"You little beast," said Antoinette, loosening her grip on Shnike in her anger, "I hate you."

The cat, seizing his opportunity, twisted onto his feet and escaped. I grabbed him as he streaked past me.

"You don't hate your sister," said Mum, "that's not a nice way to talk."

I tipped Shnike onto his back and ran my fingers through his white tummy fur. Instead of purring as he usually would, he hissed at me, his eye following the jerking ball of wool.

"I do too!" Antoinette murmured, lunging at the cat. During the short tussle that followed, Shnike dealt efficiently with us both. By the time he had finished we looked like we had been blackberry picking.

Mum's needles stopped clicking and she glared at us.

"Speak, Harold!" she exclaimed as the cat swaggered off.

"Speak, speak," said Dad mildly.

We three kids exchanged grins of delight, and peace was restored by our father's lack of cooperation.

"That is not what I meant, Harold," said Mum annoyed.

"Cold showers in the bush are a marvellous way to preserve the New Zealand pioneering spirit," said

Wendy Hamilton

Dad, getting the conversation back on track. He puffed out his chest and slashed an imaginary machete about. "Making-do and living off the smell of an oily rag is part of you kid's heritage."

"It's not part of my heritage," said Antoinette with heat. "I was kidnapped at birth. My heritage is castles and jewels, not hand-me-down clothes and mincemeat."

"What twaddle!" said Mum offended.

"You can pretend all you like," said Antoinette darkly, "but I know I'm adopted."

"Well, if that's true, I have no idea what that big lump was I carted around in my stomach," said Mum snippily.

"When are we going to get a better shower?" I whined, returning to my gripe. "In the winter when it's dark and raining, it's freezing and scary, especially when the wind blows the lantern out, and the possums are fighting overhead."

"She has a point," said Mum. "How long do you think we will have to live in the shack while you are building the house, Harold?"

Dad did not say anything for several minutes. During that time, he wore his thinking look. Consequently, he had our undivided attention when he at last spoke.

"Six months." A carpenter by trade, his words rang with authority and credibility.

"Six months!" exclaimed Mum, "I had no idea it would take that long! I was thinking in terms of six

Little House in the Cow Paddock

weeks!"

As if she had pushed an invisible button, Dad intoned, "everything takes ten times longer than you expect." He picked up the evening's newspaper and perused the headlines casually.

Now it was us, not Dad, who wore a thinking look. The room went very quiet as we multiplied six months by ten and divided it by twelve. My lucky strike with Antoinette was nothing compared to Mum when she finished her calculations.

"Harold!" Mum's tone of voice arrested Dad's attention. He put down the newspaper and looked at her. "I am happy to shift out to the bush. I don't mind living in a tin garage with no electricity while the house is being built." The light of battle was in Mum's eye as she spoke. "I can live with a toilet that is an outhouse over a hole in the ground, and a camp cooker as a stove. But I will NOT shower under a tree in the bush for five years!" She glanced out the ranch-slider at the many houses on the hill opposite. There was a pause as she weighed the lack of privacy in the backyard against the primitive ablutions at Mount Tiger. "If the blue gums were still here, I wouldn't dream of shifting," she said sorrowfully.

Dad, sensing his dream of living by the bush starting to slip away, acted rapidly.

"Don't worry, Dear," he said decisively, "I promise by the end of the weekend you will have a new shower."

Wendy Hamilton

The New Shower

My father always kept his promises. His word was better than a signed contract because Dad never wriggled out of a deal once he gave his word. So, on Friday evening when we headed off to the bush as we did every Friday night, in addition to all the normal stuff we took for the weekend, the car toted a trailer filled with building supplies for our new shower. The next morning Dad was up at the crack of dawn. I passed him on my way to the outhouse. He was looking thoughtfully at the ditch between the tin garage and the tiny shed Antoinette slept in.

"Good morning Dad," I said, picking my way around fresh cowpats.

Dad said nothing. Instead, he lifted his eyes from the ditch and gazed like a blind man into the distance. I left my father to his thoughts, picked up a small rock and continued bravely towards the toilet. At the last post of

Little House in the Cow Paddock

fresh air, I took a deep breath (like a Scooba diver) and flung open the rickety door. A huge spider scuttled into the corner of the shelf the toilet seat sat on. I squashed it with the rock and (still holding my breath) stepped inside and shut the door. The experience was like sitting in the case of an Egyptian Mummy. I did not stay a second longer than necessary. My face was blue when I burst out the door and drew a deep breath.

"Did you manage to hold your breath the whole time?" called Antoinette, poking her head out of her shed.

"Still sucking fresh air deep into my lungs, I nodded, as I lathered my hands with a weather-beaten chunk of soap and rinsed them in a nearby bucket of water.

"Yesterday, I ran out of breath before I got out," said Antoinette, tightening the floppy tie of her pink bathrobe. "Believe me, if you suspect you can't last the whole distance, it is better to take small shallow breaths." She slipped her feet into her gumboots. "Did you see any spiders?" Her voice was wobbly with fear.

"It's alright," I said, "there was a big one but I got him."

"Thanks," said Antoinette "I owe you one."

"There is a dead thrush behind the long-drop," I said shuddering.

"I'm onto it," said Antoinette. The family princess stomped around to the back of the outhouse, picked up the carcass and biffed it over the fence into the bush. "Here goes," she said, taking a deep breath before disappearing into the tall thin shed.

I shook my hands dry and wandered back towards the garage.

"What are you doing, Dad?" I asked, noting he had moved into the taking measurements phase. He stretched the tape measure between the two buildings and wrote a figure on a notepad before answering.

"That will work," he said, straightening up. He pressed a button and the steel tape whizzed back into its case.

"What will work?"

"This is the perfect spot for our new shower," said Dad, standing in the ditch and stretching out his arms. "I'll use these walls," his left hand touched the garage, his right touched Antoinette's shed, "block in one end, put a door on the other, and a lean-to-roof on top."

I heard the rattly sound of the garage door opening seconds before Mum yelled, "breakfast."

"Coming," Dad and I yelled in unison.

The door of the outhouse bashed open and Antoinette burst out, blue in the face and sucking air like an expiring fish.

"I'll be there in a second," she gasped between big gulps.

When we were all seated around the table, Dad said, "I will need everyone's help with the shower this morning." He picked up an almost empty box of cornflakes and emptied the dregs into his plate.

"A proper shower at last," beamed Mum, pulling a

Little House in the Cow Paddock

new box of cornflakes out of the cupboard. She slit the top open and sliced the inner bag. "Whose turn is it for the free gift?" she asked.

"Mine," I said in excitement. All talk of the shower was suspended as we gazed at the small packet she handed me.

"What is it this time, Wend?" said Antoinette, "is it as good as the racing car?"

"Better," I said, peering at the tiny kit set, "it's a circus elephant."

"Ooh, that's cool," said Antoinette, "look at the little wheel underneath and the umbrella in its hand, I think it is supposed to run along a thread."

"Yeah, as if it was walking a tightrope," said Rubella.

"Don't make it up now, eat your breakfast," said Mum, as I broke the pieces out of its surrounding frame and started slotting them together.

"Aw Mum," I whined, "it won't take long."

"Oh, I suppose so," said Mum giving in.

Within minutes I had it clicked together.

"As I was saying," said Dad, pouring milk over his cornflakes, "I will need everyone's help this morning to unload the trailer."

We sighed and nodded as we ate. The worst part about improvements was they did not happen by magic.

"We can leave the dishes until later for a special treat," said Mum brightly, stacking the dirty plates on the sink bench.

"Special treat indeed!" said Antoinette with a snort.

Wendy Hamilton

"Here goes," said Antoinette taking a big breath.

Little House in the Cow Paddock

"My real family would give me Belgium chocolates for a special treat," she grumbled, "they wouldn't expect me to lug heavy stuff up the hill."

"For silly talk, Lady Antoinette, not only will you help with the dishes and unloading the trailer, you will clean the toilet too," said Mum, even more brightly.

Rubella and I stifled smiles. If Mum caught us gloating, we also would be given another job.

"Right let's get on with it," said Dad, pushing his chair back and standing up.

We followed him like ducks in a line down to the car and trailer parked on the gravel track.

"Perhaps you could drive the car up the hill," suggested Mum, looking at all the lumber and corrugated iron.

Dad rubbed his chin and dug the heel of his boot into the ground. The heel sunk deep into the soft earth.

"Too wet," he said, shaking his head, "I'd get the car bogged for sure. It won't take long."

Antoinette and I exchanged suspicious glances; we had heard this type of fairy story before. He fiddled about with the rope, loosening complex knots. "Rubella, see those battens," he said, nodding towards a pile of old fence battens under the Puriri tree, "start carrying them up."

Rubella's shoulders slumped and, feet dragging, she trailed over to the pile and picked batten off the top.

"They are not heavy take two at a time," said Dad, throwing the rope clear of the trailer. Rubella did as she

Wendy Hamilton

was told and Dad handed Mum a long piece of timber. "That's better," said Dad, as she picked up a second batten.

Mum, taking the timber from him with two hands, followed Rubella up the hill.

"Wendy and Antoinette, come and take an end of this each," said Dad, lifting up a sheet of iron and sliding it partway off the trailer. Antoinette and I grabbed it and staggered up the hill awkwardly.

"Where do you want it?" I asked grumpily.

"I don't know what you're peeved about?" said Mum over her shoulder. "You are the one who started all the fuss about the shower."

"Stack it behind Antoinette's shed," said Dad.

The hands of Dad's watch snailed around the dial as we yoyoed up and down the hill like beasts of burden. At last everything was assembled, and we were rewarded with our special treat. I washed the dishes, Antoinette dried, and Rubella put them away. Meanwhile, Dad, with Mum's help, built the two end walls of our new shower.

"I hope we won't be needed again," said Rubella as a heavy piece of lumber thumped against the outside wall.

"Yeah," I agreed, looking nervously at the rafter above me. The tilly-lantern hanging off a four-inch nail quivered with every bang of Dad's hammer.

"It's a mistake to finish the dishes too quickly," said Rubella wisely, "we'll only get another job."

Little House in the Cow Paddock

Antoinette and I, recognising the pure genius of her statement, dragged the job out like an elastic band.

Mum's head popped in the door. "What's taking you so long?" she said impatiently. "When you have finished the dishes, Dad needs your help again."

"Do we have to?" we moaned.

"Don't be so lazy. It will be worth it all when you have a proper shower tonight," said Mum ignoring our grumbles. She went back to help Dad and we stumped reluctantly behind her. Things had progressed rapidly while we dillydallied. The framework was up and the end wall enclosed. Dad, holding a crumbling fence batten, stood straddled across the ditch.

"Rubella and Antoinette, I want you to lay these across the ditch to make a floor," said Dad laying three side by side, so the girls could see exactly what he wanted. "Now you do it."

Rubella and Antoinette pulled a face and did what they were told as Dad swung up into the rafters.

"Wendy, help your mother hand me up a sheet of iron," he said, taking a nail out of his builder's apron and sliding his hammer out of the belt. As Mum and I hoisted the iron up, a small breeze caught the edge pushing us backwards. We staggered about until we got it under control and dropped the end on the edge of the end rafter. Dad caught it, pulled it into place, and secured it with hard-hitting bangs.

My father was right about everything taking ten times longer than you expect. The shadows were

Wendy Hamilton

lengthening by the time the building was finished. We left Dad to the mysteries of plumbing while Mum made dinner, and Antoinette cleaned the toilet. Rubella and I lay slumped on our beds.

"That was hard work," said Rubella.

"Yeah, but it will be worth it," I said, forgetting the labour of the day in my anticipation of a hot shower.

Dad popped his head in the door. His face beamed with the satisfaction of a job well done. "Who wants to be the first to have a proper shower?" he said jovially. "It's all set up and ready to go."

"Meeee," I yelled.

Rubella glared at me.

"Why do you get to go first?" she said jealously.

"Because I'm the eldest," I smirked. As I walked out into the dark night, I noticed with satisfaction the wind was getting up. It made the pleasure of a proper shower all the greater. This is so much better than showering under the tree in the bush, I thought, opening the tidy door between the big and little shed. A pool of yellow flickering light spread over the batten floor and around the mismatched walls. All was pleasant until my gaze lifted higher; dangling from the rafters, on a heavy chain, was the familiar old watering can! I tilted it forward suspiciously, and cold water sprayed out. So much for a proper shower.

"How was it?" said Rubella, as I came back inside after the ordeal.

"Horrible," I said in broken tones. As I lay in bed

Little House in the Cow Paddock

trying to warm up, I played with the wheel of my little circus elephant. I could hear Antoinette's shrieks through the wall as she endured her proper shower.

Thank goodness Mum and Dad were not in charge of choosing the special treats dispensed by the cornflakes box.

Wendy Hamilton

Shovels, Picks and a Concrete floor.

"I thought we would have sold the house by now," said Mum with disappointment in her voice. She was seated in her armchair with her feet up and perusing a telephone book. "It's been a month and still nothing."

"Everything takes ten times longer than you expect," said Dad automatically. He sat at the table adding up long columns of figures.

"Perhaps I should list it as a dual agency?" said Mum, glancing out the ranch-slider at the hundred houses on the hill.

"Good idea," murmured Dad vaguely, as he opened a bank book and wrote down another figure.

"Two agents might be better than one," said Mum nibbling a fingernail. "I don't like to tell our agent he's

Little House in the Cow Paddock

getting competition." She sighd. "He is a lovely little man, so quiet."

"Perhaps that's his problem," said Dad, looking in another bank book and frowning. "Are these two bank books all we have?" he asked in a worried tone.

"No," said Mum, turning to the yellow pages, "there are another six in the junk drawer."

"Wendy, can you get them for me please," said Dad.

"Why do parents always make it sound like you have a choice," I muttered under my breath in annoyance as I put down the cat. Immediately, Antoinette pounced on him as I knew she would.

I walked through to the kitchen and rummaged in the junk drawer.

"You're in my way," said Rubella, elbowing me.

"Umm, does Mum know what you're doing?" I asked in a singsong voice, looking at a line of yoghurt pottles and ice cream containers sitting on the bench; they were filled with dirt and straggly ferns.

"She won't mind," said Rubella brazenly.

"Mum," I called softly, shooting a glance at Rubella from the corner of my eye.

"Shut up," hissed Rubella, her bravado crumpling.

"Didn't Mum say you couldn't have any more plants after the rubber plant rotted the carpet in your bedroom?"

"She said if I bought any more ferns, she would stop my pocket money," said Rubella. "I haven't bought these, I found them behind the stone wall and under the

Wendy Hamilton

trees by the creek."

"I don't think it will make any difference," I said, "Mum is still going to be mad about more plants."

"She won't notice," said Rubella, turning on the sink tap and dribbling water into each pot.

"Humph," I snorted, "you're right about that, there are so many in there it looks like you are sleeping in a fernery."

"It does not," said Rubella with heat, "I've got cactuses and succulents as well."

"You'd better put plates under them all," I sniggered, pointing to the growing pools of muddy water leaking onto the bench, "or Mum will get really mad."

"What's taking you so long, Wendy?" called Dad.

Rubella poked her tongue out at me and I poked mine back at her, as I grabbed the bank books and ran through to the lounge.

"Here you are," I said, dumping them on the table. "What are you doing?"

"I'm working out how much it would cost to lay the floor of our new house," said Dad, shuffling papers. "These are quotes for steel and concrete." He opened the rest of the bank books and continued writing figures and adding up columns.

"I think I'll try this agency," said Mum, circling a half-page add, "the lady has a nice face."

I sat on the floor and Antoinette generously let me have half of the cat. I tickled one half of his tummy and she tickled the other half. The cat, in a mellow mood,

Little House in the Cow Paddock

lay with his paws in the air, purring and waving the tip of his tail lazily.

Dad stopped writing, looked up and cleared his throat. "As I see it, Anne," he said looking at Mum, "we don't have to wait until this house is sold to make a start on the new one."

"Really?" said Mum, happily.

"Yes," nodded Dad. "If we use rocks from our quarry and do all the work ourselves, we have enough money to put down the concrete floor."

Antoinette and I exchanged nervous glances.

"I don't like the sound of doing all the work," I whispered over the cat's stomach.

Antoinette grimaced and nodded.

"Oh, Harold, how wonderful," said Mum beaming. "When can we start?"

"This weekend," said Dad.

A man of his word, Dad was up early on Saturday morning marking out the L shaped floor with string lines. That part was pleasant, and interesting, and did not involve us. Even digging the turf off the ground (which did involve us) was not too bad. From there on in, it got increasingly horrible.

"It's Murphies Law we have a property with a small quarry on it," I said bitterly, swinging a pickaxe into the red rock. "The chances of that must be a million to one."

"A beastly jackpot to win," grumbled Rubella, lifting a big rock and dumping it into the trailer.

Wendy Hamilton

We went back and forth from the trailer to the house site.

Little House in the Cow Paddock

"My real family would never expect me to quarry rock," moaned Antoinette, glaring at our parents who were working hard a small distance away. She put down her huge spade and examined her hands. "My nails are chipped and I have blisters on blisters."

"I don't think it's fair that Mum has a lady's spade," whined Rubella. "Why couldn't we all have a small lightweight one like hers?"

"Seriously, Rubella, would you really want Dad to buy you a spade for *your* birthday?" I said. "I'd rather have a new bridle for Wuzzel."

"Not if that was the only way to get one," said Rubella, seeing things in a new light, she picked up her huge spade and dug a teaspoon of gravel out of the ground. "I'd rather have a scooter."

"Pick up your spade and keep working, Antoinette," called Dad. Some black magic (linked to work) had turned our mild-mannered father into a slave driver. We continued working and grumbling. We fussed as we picked at the stone. We moaned as we levered rocks. We griped as we dug gravel. Fussing, moaning, and griping, got us through the ordeal. It is marvellous how suffering increases comradery. Antoinette, Rubella, and I, got through the whole morning without a single fight.

"That will do," said Dad, calling a halt at last.

Mum and Dad got into the car while we scrambled onto the trailer and perched uncomfortably on the knobbly rocks.

"The trailer ride is the only good part," said

Wendy Hamilton

Antoinette.

We nodded and clung on as Dad drove slowly out of the quarry, along the gravel track, past the Puriri tree, through the gate, past the patch where Antoinette's shed used to sit, around the corner, through the gate, into the next paddock, and over to the building site.

"I wish it were longer," I said, as we climbed stiffly down.

Unloading was mildly better than digging for rocks. We yo-yoed back and forth from the trailer to the house-site dumping rocks and gravel in the big bald L. Dad meanwhile, did complicated things with his tape measure and string lines to ensure we got everything level.

That was how were spent every Saturday morning for a long time. Our joy at the end of the quarrying was cut short, however, when we found ourselves under a hot sun, tying steel mesh to metal rods with thin wire. Then at last the nightmare was over.

"The way I see concrete is forever changed," moaned Antoinette, banging the door of the garage shut on our first weekend of freedom. "I know far more about concrete than I ever wanted to."

We walked towards the grey slab lying a short distance away.

"The concrete truck was exciting," said Rubella, as we climbed a wire fence.

"Yeah, that was the only good part," I said. "That was really fun. The best part was watching all those

Little House in the Cow Paddock

men working and not having to do a thing ourselves."

"No," said Antoinette, sitting on the edge of the concrete floor and pulling on her skates, "the best part is having our own private skating rink. Not even Meagan has one of those."

Wendy Hamilton

A Horse for Free

It was the school holidays. Skylarks warbled as they dipped and climbed in the sapphire sky. Mason bees droned as they built their homes of mud in the nooks and crannies of the shed at Mount Tiger. The big garage door was wide open, and Antoinette's transistor radio sat on the table.

"Ooh, ooh, heart of glass," it sang in a cheap, made-in-china voice.

Dad was not on holiday. He was at work, inspecting houses and hauling shoddy builders off to court. With him out of the way, life sank into comfortable laziness. Mum sat on her bed knitting, while Rubella lolled on the floor playing with the cat. Within poking distance, Antoinette peered into the cracked and spotty mirror on the wall as she experimented with a sample pack of eye shadow. I lounged on my homemade bunk with a book. As I read, I sucked boiled sweets secretly because

Little House in the Cow Paddock

I did not want to share. Near to the open door my horse, Wuzzel, cropped grass and munched noisily, her feet making slow plonks as she moved slowly forward. It was all very pleasant and ordinary until she decided to join us.

"Oh here!" Mum exclaimed, dropping a stitch as Wuzzel stomped in and sat her saggy muzzle on top of the transistor radio. "Get that animal out of here."

"Aw Mum do I have to?" I pleaded, thrilled by this unexpected visitor, "she likes the music."

"Yeah, she does," said Antoinette, turning around and looking at Wuzzel through eyes ringed with mismatched colours.

"She likes it so much she is going to sleep," said Rubella.

"Yeah, and look at her ears, they've gone all floppy with happiness," I agreed.

"Get that animal out before she poops on the carpet," said Mum, unmoved.

"It's only an old carpet square."

"I don't care," said Mum, "and don't say, 'it is only a polythene sheet and an earth floor underneath,'" continued Mum, reading my mind, "it doesn't make any difference."

"Come on Wuzzel," I said, slipping down from my bunk, "you've got to go outside," I pushed on her chest and she backed slowly out. "I would let you stay but some people (I looked at Mum meaningfully) don't want you."

Wendy Hamilton

Once she was out, I climbed back onto the top bunk and gazed out the grimy window, noting idly the big spider in the corner of the pane. Wuzzel, meanwhile, hung around the shed munching grass and listening to the Top Ten songs until the program changed to a talkback show.

"I think Wuzzel is lonely," I said, watching her drift down the hill to join the cattle grazing by the spring. "Horses are herd animals so she needs a friend."

"No more animals we can't sell to the meatworks," said Mum. "I don't know what we are going to do about that stroppy sheep, it was terrible the way he bailed Mr. Walters up when he came around and we were not here."

"I'm amazed Mr. Walters can still climb a tree," I said giggling. "I thought he was too old for that sort of thing."

Mum gave me THE LOOK, and I immediately stopped giggling.

"It is astonishing what the human body can do when fear pumps enough adrenalin through it," she said switching off THE LOOK, "even when it is over seventy."

"Larry is not scary," said Rubella.

"He can be, when he is in his bunting mood," said Antoinette, recalling the many times we had been knocked over.

"Larry wouldn't have chased him under normal circumstances," I said. As the one who brought the pet sheep for Rubella's birthday, I felt my reputation was

Little House in the Cow Paddock

under attack. "It's only because Mr. Walters had his spaniel with him. Larry can't help it if he was raised by an Alsatian and lived in a kennel when he was a lamb!"

"Can we have a dog?" said Rubella.

"Absolutely not," said Mum in horrified tones.

"Meagan has a purebred poodle," said Antoinette, painting green streaks above her purple eyelids. "It's won so many shows Meagan has a whole wall covered in ribbons."

"Has it won any cups and trophies?" asked Rubella.

"So many cups her mother uses them at parties as goblets for wine," drawled Antoinette in a posh voice.

"I don't think so, Antoinette," said Mum in a squashing tone. "Don't let your imagination carry you away."

"Well, Meagan and I drank fizz out of one of them," pouted Antoinette, in her normal voice, "and that's the honest truth."

The conversation continued in this manner, moving further and further away from Wuzzel's loneliness. The idea of a companion for her might not have been raised again if it weren't for the ad in the paper a few weeks later.

"Mum there is a horse for free in the paper," I said in excitement.

"Did you say for free?" said Antoinette pricking her ears, she was lying on her stomach in the lounge, pretending to do her homework. Unlike Rubella, who couldn't be bothered with horses, Antoinette was

Wendy Hamilton

smitten with horse fever. "If we got another one, we wouldn't have to double on Wuzzel all the time."

"Yes," I said, pinching a pen from her pencil case and circling the ad. I leaned on the side of my mother's armchair and thrust the paper at her, "see Mum."

"Hang on a minute," said Mum, wrinkling her brow as she concentrated on a tricky part in her knitting pattern. "Knit one, purl one, slip four onto another needle, knit four…"

"Horse FREE to a good home." I paused and looked expectantly at my mother.

"Twist and knit four stitches, purl one…" said Mum under her breath.

I raised my voice and tried again. All I needed was Mum's Scottish heritage to activate. "Horse FREE… FREEEEEE…" I lingered on the magic word and at last I got a strike.

Mum jerked her head up."What's free?"

"There's a horse in the paper free to a good home," I said pointing at the classified ad. "Wuzzel is lonely and needs a paddock mate."

"A free horse?" said Mum, I could almost (but not quite) hear her mother's Scotch accent in her voice.

"Yup. 'Horse free to a good home. 18 years old, ex stock horse, very quiet phone 439, triple six, 82,'" I read aloud.

Mum whisked the paper out of my hand and scooted through to the hallway, where the telephone sat in spender on its own special table. I followed her and

Little House in the Cow Paddock

hovered nearby, eavesdropping as she made the call. I did not need both sides of the conversation to glean it was going well, so well, Mrs Childs arranged for us to meet her and Pretty Lady after school the next day.

The farm where they lived was thirty miles away. Mum pulled into the driveway and stopped outside a weatherboard farmhouse. In the garden was an elderly muscular woman.

"Hello, you must be Anne," she said to Mum, as we got out.

"Yes, and you must be Mrs. Childs," said Mum.

"Come this way," said Mrs. Childs taking off her gardening gloves and putting them in a nearby bucket. We followed her as she led the way to a paddock by a shearing shed.

"This is Pretty Lady," she said as a fifteen-hand high horse with a bushy mane and kind eyes plodded towards us.

"Hello Pretty Lady," I said, handing her a carrot and stroking her dark nose sprinkled with grey hairs.

"Why does her tail look like that?" asked Rubella, looking at the fuzzy bottle-brush hanging off Pretty Lady's ample rear end.

"The calves ate it," smiled Mrs Childs, laying a hand on the horse's neck. "She let them because she thought she was their mother. I raised her from a foal and hate to see her go," she said in a wobbly voice, "but I'm shifting into town. A retirement village is no place for a horse." Her eyes glazed as she gazed into the distance of yesteryears. "When it was shearing time, and I couldn't steer her because my hands were full of scones and buns for the shearers, Pretty Lady didn't know what I wanted, so she went around the paddock rounding up all the cows."

"She is beautiful," said Antoinette sincerely, the pride of ownership glowing in her eyes (because it was agreed Pretty Lady was to be hers.)

As Mum and Mrs Childs got better acquainted, we made friends with Pretty Lady. It was not difficult to love her. She was a lovely natured horse. She did not have the worldly suspicious mind of Wuzzel, who had endured many kids and pony clubs. By the time we left it was all settled. We would pick Pretty Lady up on Saturday morning, and Mrs Childs could come to our place and ride her whenever she liked.

Little House in the Cow Paddock

The Trip Home

Pretty Lady had led a sheltered life on the farm of her birth. She had never been in a horse trailer or seen more than two cars on a road. Mrs. Childs was all for riding her to Mount Tiger but it was impossible to avoid a stretch of a busy highway. So that was the end of that idea.

"There is nothing for it, we'll have to hire a horse trailer," said my father when he heard the problem.

That Friday night, instead of going out to Mount Tiger as we usually did, we stayed in town. The night was beastly as I was too excited to sleep and time crawled. Fortunately, everything comes to an end eventually, and at last we were at the Hire Center.

"Are you sure those are horse floats?" I asked Dad, as he slowed the car to a halt beside a line of narrow windowless trailers, "they look like they are made for moving pianos."

Wendy Hamilton

"The guy in the office said they were," said Dad, getting out and hooking one onto our tow bar. He screwed the safety chain on before getting back in the car.

"It feels very light," he said, driving out the gate.

The trailer bounced behind us like a cereal box on wheels as we drove through town and out to the country. If I thought it looked strange, my response was nothing compared to Pretty Lady's reaction when we rattled into the driveway. She looked at the contraption as if it were an alien spaceship. Her alarm grew as Dad lowered the back into a ramp and Mrs. Childs led her towards it.

"Come on girl," soothed Mrs. Childs, coaxing her in with carrots, "it's all right."

Pretty lady was not convinced. Her big black eyes were ringed with white, her head was high, and her neck rigid. But trust and obedience inched her stiff-legged up the ramp. When the last of Pretty lady quivered into place, Dad swung up the ramp and shut her in as Mrs. Childs popped out the small door at the front. The trailer, now filled with horse, looked even narrower. Pretty Lady's rump rose above the sides like the top of a muffin, and her fuzzy tail hung over the back like a woolly duster.

"Everybody into the car," said Dad, shooting the bolts on the ramp home.

"Goodbye, Pretty Lady," quavered Mrs. Childs wiping her eyes, as Dad drove slowly out the driveway and along the road.

Little House in the Cow Paddock

The journey at first was not too bad. Pretty Lady coped with the unfamiliar movement remarkably well. She even managed the main road without fussing.

"This is so much easier than when we got Wuzzel," Antoinette said.

I nodded in agreement. "Much quicker than walking for three days."

"Here we go, this could be tricky," said Mum, nervously biting her nails as we entered the outskirts of town. But even as the traffic thickened and cars whizzed on either side of us, Pretty Lady stayed quiet.

"This is going better than I expected," said Dad in a relieved tone.

"Yeah," I said, noticing the envious girl in a passing car. I sat up straighter, "much better. This is actually fun."

Two more heads turned and I sat even higher. By the time we stopped at the lights I was sitting so tall I was almost standing. The girl in the car alongside craned her neck to get a glimpse of our horse and my joy was complete.

"I bet that girl wishes she was us," I said in an English accent.

"Yeah, I bet she does," said Antoinette. The lights turned green and my body and voice returned to normal as we moved forward and lost sight of her.

"Well, we are through the worst "said Dad, as we drove past the houseboats in the mangroves and headed out of town.

Wendy Hamilton

He spoke too soon. As we breasted the Onerahi hill, Pretty Lady went wild.

"What is happening?" said Dad, flicking his eyes back and forth between the road and the rear vision mirror.

"It's Pretty lady," I screamed, panicking. "She's trying to climb out!"

Dad pulled to the side of the road and we burst out of the car and rushed around to the trailer. Pretty Lady's rump and head rose and fell as the big animal thrashed about in the confined space. Her shifting weight rocked the trailer and bounced the stationary car. My father, who could fix any problem, stood scratching his head with his mouth hanging open. Angels (or so it seemed) in the form of two old blokes came to our rescue. One of them hobbled on bow legs over to the small side door, opened it, and fearlessly popped his head inside.

"Wow girl, easy does it," he soothed in a calm voice.

The other man hopped up onto the mudguard and stroked the heaving back. "Steady, steady," he drawled.

Pretty Lady's nose was bleeding and her eyes were wild. But as the men talked, the whites of her eyes shrunk and eventually disappeared as her eyelids lowered.

"That's better, nothing's going to harm you," said Bow Legs, catching hold of Pretty Lady's halter and stepping bravely inside. It was obvious to us all (including Pretty Lady) Bow Legs knew a lot about horses. As he calmed and petted her, Pretty Lady's neck relaxed, her head went down, and she stood still. In

Little House in the Cow Paddock

response, the car stopped bucking, and the throbbing of my heart slowed to normal.

"You'll be right now," said Bow legs, climbing out the little door and shutting it quietly behind him.

"I can't thank you enough," gushed Mum, "you were wonderful."

"Yes, that was marvellous," said Dad, shaking their hands, "thank you for all your help."

"How far have you got to go?" asked Mudguard Man.

"About ten miles," said Dad, "we're on our way to Mount Tiger."

"She'll be OK now," nodded Bow Legs confidently.

And he was right. Pretty Lady shuffled a bit as we wound along the waterfront, but that was all. Once we turned inland and the car started climbing up the hills, things went completely quiet.

"That's strange, I can't feel the trailer pulling me about," said Dad, uncertain whether or not to be pleased.

"Oh no, she's died," I moaned in horror.

"Don't be such a drama queen, Wendy," said Mum, fear making her tone sharp.

In low ear, our poor car laboured up and down the ever-rising hills. Unbeknown to us at the time, the violent shaking it received, had broken something underneath. Despite being wounded, it dragged its heavy burden up punishing inclines like a faithful little trooper, until it clanked through our gate. As the car rolled to a halt, we heaved a sigh of relief. Even then our ordeal was not entirely over. We tumbled out of the doors and watched nervously as Dad loosened the bolts that held the ramp shut.

"At least she is still alive," said Rubella looking at Pretty Lady's rump, "if she was dead, she would be slumped against the side."

"Stand back," warned Dad, "she might rush out when the door goes down."

We moved a safe distance away as Dad let down the ramp, taking care to stand well to the side.

We all held our breath as it fell onto the ground with a loud bang. To our surprise, Pretty Lady did nothing.

"If a horse dies when it is standing up, perhaps it doesn't fall over," I wailed, "a table isn't alive but it stands up."

"Her ears are moving," said Antoinette, creeping forward.

We waited until impatience demanded action. Dad opened the little door at the front and stepped in bravely. Still nothing happened.

"Come on Pretty Lady," we called encouragingly as he pushed her gently backwards. The chunky horse came out slowly, one step at a time.

Wuzzel, in the neighbouring paddock, saw the back end of a horse. She pricked up her ears and let out a throaty whinny as she trotted back and forth along the fence line.

"Wendy, you'd better catch Wuzzel and keep her out of the way until we get through," said Dad, as Antoinette

Little House in the Cow Paddock

clipped a lead rope onto Pretty Lady's halter. "We'll never get the gate open otherwise."

I climbed the wire fence and caught Wuzzel's halter with a trembling hand. "I hate the horse welcoming-ritual," I muttered under my breath. "Come on girl," I said loudly, dragging her away from the gate with difficulty, "you can meet Pretty Lady soon."

Once we were out of the way, Antoinette led Pretty Lady through the gate, and Dad shut it behind them.

"OK," Antoinette called, unclipping the rope and letting her go. Pretty Lady, looking rather dazed, trotted a wee way off.

"You can let Wuzzel go now, Wendy," called Dad.

I took my hand off Wuzzel's halter and she and I shot opposite directions. She galloped over to her new friend while I scarpered over to the fence and scaled it in record time. As usual, there was a lot of nose sniffing and prancing, head tossing and squealing.

"Let's leave them to sort themselves out," said Dad, shutting the ramp with a bang, "I have to have this trailer back by twelve, I don't want to pay hiring fees for the whole day. Who wants to come with Mum and me for a ride into town?"

"Me," said Rubella, climbing back into the car.

"I'll stay here," I said.

"So will I," said Antoinette.

"There are cans of food under the bed," said Mum, "open some baked beans or something for lunch. I'll bring bread with me when we come back. See you in an hour." She slammed the door of the car shut.

We waved until the car disappeared from sight before drifting towards the fence.

"You remember when I said 'getting Pretty Lady was much easier than getting Wuzzel?'" said Antoinette, as we hung over the gate and watched the two horses squeal and nip. "I've changed my mind."

"Yeah," I agreed, "three days of walking was heaps easier."

Little House in the Cow Paddock

Hidden Treasure.

"Three months and still no buyers," said Mum. She did not bother to look out the ranch-slider as she spoke, because by now the sight of a hundred houses on the hill was familiar. "I'm going to list the house with every agent in town."

"Good idea," said Dad vaguely. Once again, he was seated at the dining room table surrounded by bank books.

"Sales pick up in October," said Mum hopefully.

"Hmm," said Dad, tapping his calculator busily.

"October is a nice settled month," continued Mum, "not too hot, not too cold, and not so much rain."

Dad stopped tapping and wrote a figure in his notebook. "You'll be pleased to know," he said beaming at Mum, "we have enough money to put up the frame of the house."

"Oh Doggal, how wonderful!"

Wendy Hamilton

Antoinette, Rubella, and I, exchanged nervous glances.

"That's the end of our lazy weekends," I whispered anxiously.

"Yeah, back to slavery," said Antoinette.

In life, things you wait for seldom live up to expectations, even nasty things. It turned out our fears were unfounded. Building the framework of the house required the sort of skills only my father had. A big truck delivered a huge pile of timber, and every Saturday Dad ut on his builder's apron and went to work, while the rest of us lazed and played.

"Now I know why they say ignorance is bliss," I said to Antoinette, as we wandered along the track to the quarry.

"Ignorance has a lot going for it," she agreed, picking up a stick and slashing at a tall thistle.

We rounded the corner and passed through the narrow entrance into the quarry. It fanned out before us; a hidden little world all of its own. Thick bush hugged the outer left edge that dropped steeply into the gully, while the bank on our right side turned into a curving wall of rock, as the hill rose but the quarry floor did not.

"I'm glad all that hideous quarrying is over, playing horse shows is much more fun," I said, getting down to business.

"This will make a nice arena," said Antoinette, surveying the round flat area thoughtfully

"That can be the judge's stand," I said pointing to

Little House in the Cow Paddock

the highest spot of the cliff face. "Rubella will be able to see everything from there."

"Yeah, and it's far enough away from the toilet and the fly-bottle, not to stink too much," said Antoinette practically.

"Let's move some of these bigger rocks out of the way," I said, looking at a few big rocks scattered around, "they could be dangerous."

The idea seemed good to Antoinette, so we each picked a stone and rolled it over the edge. Mine bounced down the hill in a series of dull thumps, but Antoinette's crashed, banged, and pinged, in the most interesting manner. Antoinette pushed into the tea-tree and peered down the hill. "Hey Wend, there's an old dump down here," she shouted.

"Really?"

"Yeah, really!" She grasped the soft black trunk of a tea tree and eased herself carefully down the slippery slope. "I can see some old bottles."

"Are any of them blue?" I asked, grabbing trees and scrambling after her.

"Yeah, and some green ones too."

The dump was only a little distance down the hill. I could hear Dad's hammer banging as Antoinette and I trawled through tin cans and old boots looking for treasure. We each found several bottles (filled with dirt and only slightly chipped) and a few jam jars. Antoinette found a dented enamel jug and a cow's skull. But I stumbled across the best treasure of all.

Wendy Hamilton

"Look at this," I crowed, pulling a banjo ukulele out from under an old oilskin coat.

"Wow, Wend, that is neat," said Antoinette, genuinely pleased for me. "Do you think it is played the same way as an ordinary ukulele?"

"I would imagine so," I said, tightening the only string. I pinged it and it made a tinny banjo noise. "It looks the same size as my ukulele," I said excitedly, "I'll swap the strings onto it and see what it sounds like."

"Let's take this stuff back," said Antoinette, "you go up and I'll hand everything to you. It would be easier that way."

"Good idea." I held my treasure in one hand and with the other I grabbed trees and hauled myself up and onto the quarry floor. Then I leaned down and Antoinette handed me the rest of the stuff.

"Pass me that old coat," I said, as she handed me the last item, "we can use it as a bag."

Antoinette nodded, pulled it out of the pile and clambered up to meet me. It was very quiet all of a sudden, the steady banging had stopped.

"It must be lunchtime," I said as we laid our stuff on the coat.

"I'll come back for the cow's skull later," said Antoinette, looking at the pile on the oilskin. She tied the sleeves together to make a handle while I picked up the hem with two hands.

"Yeah, there's not enough room for it," I said, as we shuffled forward, "and I don't think Mum will let you

Little House in the Cow Paddock

keep it. Remember what happened to the last one."

"I'm older now, I won't use her toothbrush to clean this one's teeth," said Antoinette, with the wisdom of hindsight. "I'll get it later and hide it under my bed. Promise you won't say anything about it?"

"I promise," I said, as we stumbled along the gravel track and up the hill to the garage.

Mum had lunch on the table by the time we stashed our horde in Antoinette's shed and washed our hands.

"How's the building going?" said Mum, after Dad had given thanks for the food.

"Very good," said Dad, buttering two slices of bread, "I've got the frames of the outer walls done."

"That's marvellous," said Mum, pouring out a cup of tea.

"I'll need a hand lifting them up this afternoon," said Dad, spreading Marmite on his sandwich.

I groaned and pulled a face. Mum gave me THE LOOK.

"Don't be so lazy, Wendy, you kids haven't helped for weeks."

"It won't take long," said Dad.

I did not believe him but I said nothing, because Mum's eye was still upon me.

"I found a dump," said Antoinette proudly. THE LOOK disappeared from Mum's face as everyone's attention shifted to Antoinette.

Wendy Hamilton

I found the best treasure of all.

Little House in the Cow Paddock

"Did you?"

"Yes," she said, puffing out her chest and swelling with importance, "and it's on our land so it belongs to us. The Council can't stop us from taking stuff out of it."

"It's really mean of the Council to do that," said Rubella pouting, "last time we went to the dump I found a big stack of plastic plant pots, but the man wouldn't let me take them."

"I saw a really nice sewing basket," I said, leaping in on the conversation, "the handles were a bit wobbly but other than that it was perfectly alright. I nearly cried when the bulldozer ran it over. It was such a waste."

"Tell us about going to the dump when you were a boy, Dad," Antoinette said without a trace of an English accent. Even Lady Antoinette found it impossible to reject her heritage when it came to fossicking through dumps.

"When we were kids," said Dad, starting a well-worn story, "you could take whatever you wanted from the dump."

We gasped with envy, even Mum, on account of her Scottish blood.

"We had a saying, 'half a load to the dump and a full load home," said Dad. "We used to get old canvas and bamboo sticks from the dump and make them into canoes then we floated them down the Rangatiki river."

"What about the timber you got for your tree hut," I prompted him, taking a bite of a peanut butter sandwich.

Wendy Hamilton

"No, that didn't come from the dump," Dad corrected me, taking a sip of tea. "I prayed for that for several weeks, and one morning I got up and there was all this timber in our backyard. The first miracle was the neighbour had demolished the fence. The second miracle was I saw it first and bagsed it, that was the way we did things in my family."

"Was that when you decided to become a builder?"

"I can't remember," said Dad. "My father was a builder, and I've always been good with my hands, so it seemed natural. Building's part of your heritage. Speaking of which, it's high time you all learnt to drive in a four-inch nail."

"What?" I said in alarm. "But I'm just a little girl," whined Antoinette, digging up an old phrase for the emergency.

"Stop whining, Antoinette," said Mum frowning, "you're not five anymore."

"No," agreed Antoinette bitterly, "but I am a girl. Girls don't build."

"Nonsense," said Dad, "girls can do anything, and boys too for that matter. When I was a child money was scarce and my mother insisted that we all knew how to stuff grass into tires when the inner tube blew, and make clothes out of flour sacks."

"On Grandma's old treadle sewing machine?" I asked, thinking of the foot peddle we pumped to make train noises.

"That's the one," said Dad. He chuckled. "I

Little House in the Cow Paddock

remember onetime Ernie decided to shape his pants, and when he was finished the leg holes were the size of fifty-cent pieces."

"Ha ha," I laughed louder and longer than necessary, hoping to delay my building lesson.

"What about Auntie Rose, did she have to sew?" said Antoinette, spinning the story out.

"Oh yes, and she was good at it, but she could also knock a wheelbarrow together and get a bee's nest out of the back of a washing machine," said Dad. "We always had bees and sometimes they swarmed in awkward places."

"Bee's nests," I said, growing even more alarmed.

"Yes, and that reminds me," said Dad, "I think I saw a swarm in the bush. Beekeeping is also part of your heritage."

"Didn't you need some help with lifting up the house frame," I said desperately. Compared with collecting wild bees, building seemed tame.

"Yes," said Dad, glancing at the clock and getting up. "We'd better get on with it."

"I don't know why so many people are keen on equal rights," I grumbled to Antoinette, as we trailed out the door behind Dad.

"Beats me," said Antoinette, also mystified. "Hammers and bees! Why would any woman want to do a man's job?"

"Equal rights stink," I nodded.

Wendy Hamilton

The Frame Goes Up

We stood gathered around a wooden grid lying on the concrete floor. Dad pointed to the line of reinforcing steel poking out of the perimeter of the concrete.

"See these holes," he tapped his foot on the bottom rail of the grid. "When I say so, lift the frame and slot the rods through the holes. Got it?"

We nodded.

"On the count of three, one, two, three, lift."

We made puffing sounds of effort as we stood the wall upright, and hoisted it over the rods.

"That's it, keep holding it up," said Dad, rapidly nailing a piece of timber onto it like the leg of a tripod. "OK, that should hold it, you can let go now."

We moved onto the next wall and did the same thing.

Little House in the Cow Paddock

The visual impact of raising the frame was astonishing. By the time we had worked systematically around the edge of the floor, the house had shifted into three dimensions.

"You can all have a rest," said Dad, "but don't go away."

Mum admired the size of the house, while Dad bashed the steel over and secured it to the bottom plate with big fencing staples. Meanwhile, we three kids twirled and danced in excitement. We stopped dancing when all the corners were fused together with nails, however, because there was more work to be done.

"Bring all those trusses into the house," said Dad, pointing to a triangular pile under a nearby tree.

"I thought we were finished," I said pouting, my shoulders slumping.

"We still need a roof," said Dad.

Antoinette's pirouette flopped into flat-footed stomping and Rubella's skipping dwindled into dawdling, as we followed our parents to our next job. Then there was more hoisting as we shuffled back and forth carrying trusses. At last we were finished. Once again, we danced, and once again our dancing was cut short by weight-lifting.

"Hoist the end up and onto the top plate," said Dad.

Obediently (with much grumbling) we poked a pointy end up and onto the top of the wall.

"Now do the other side."

We did as we were told.

Wendy Hamilton

"Let's play horse and cart."

Little House in the Cow Paddock

"That looks funny," giggled Rubella, looking at the triangle hanging upside down in the house. "How is that going to be a roof?"

"You'll see," said Dad, clambering up the walls like a monkey. "It's not really a roof," he corrected, "it's the fame for the roof to sit on. Use a stick and swing the middle up."

Mum picked up a piece of timber and we lifted. Things got interesting as the triangle swivelled upwards and Dad caught it. Like a magic trick, it turned into the apex of the roof; wobbling slightly in the breeze as Dad nailed it in place.

"Harold, it doesn't look very safe," said Mum, noticing the wobble.

"It will be alright once we get two up," said Dad confidently. "Swing the next one up."

We swung and Dad caught.

"Hand me a length of timber, Wendy," said Dad, pointing to the pile below.

Stretching, I handed him one and he fastened the two trusses together with it.

"See, Anne," he said shaking them, "the more we get up here the stronger everything will be."

"Come on girls," said Mum anxiously, "let's get these up there quickly."

Suddenly things were getting exciting as bit by bit the roof grew. By nightfall we had the ghost of a house made of sticks.

Building is not all bad," I said to Antoinette the next

morning as I tightened the strings on my banjo ukulele.

"No, it's not," agreed Antoinette, settling herself in the rafters next to me. "This is a great jungle-gym."

I strummed a chord, stopped, and fiddled with the tuning knobs. Down below, Dad worked on the framework of the internal walls while Mum swept up sawdust. Meanwhile, Larry Lamb skipped and bounced behind Rubella as she skated over the smooth concrete. I strummed another chord.

"Let's sing Mockingbird Hill," I said.

"OK," said Antoinette, breaking into song.

"When the sun in the morning creeps over the hill…" we sang.

Bang, bang, bang, went Dad's hammer.

"And kisses the roses on my windowsill…"

Sweep, sweep, sweep, went Mum.

"Then my heart fills with gladness as I hear the trill…"

Skate, skate, skate, went Rubella.

"Of the birds in the treetops in Mockingbird Hill."

Boing, boing, boing, went Larry.

"Tri-la-la twiddly dee dee.." The tri-la-las were cut short as my banjo ukulele slipped out of tune.

"Hang on a minute, Noo," I said, using my sister's pet name, "I need to tighten the strings again."

Antoinette swung her legs as she waited. "Let's sing it in opera," she said, having a marvellous inspiration.

"Alright," I said, charmed at the idea. I twiddled with the pegs a bit longer. When it sounded alright, I

Little House in the Cow Paddock

started strumming again.

"When the sun in the morning…" we warbled in strange tones from the back of our throats.

We got all the way to the tri-la-las before Mum cut our performance short with an exclamation of rage.

"Look here! I'm not having that animal poop all over my nice new floor." She glared at the small raisins raining from the rear end of Larry as he bounced about.

"Aw Mum, it doesn't matter," protested Antoinette, "it's only concrete.

"I don't care," said my house-proud mother, "they will leave stains on the floor. There, see what I mean," she said, as Rubella skated over a small ball and it smeared into a long greenish-black streak.

"But they sweep up easily," she said, falling down with a bang and licking her grazed knee.

Right on cue, Larry let a long stream of steaming liquid out of the middle of his undercarriage.

"That does it," said Mum, "get that animal out of here." Moving Larry was not a one-person job. Antoinette and I climbed down the walls while Rubella took her skates off.

"Let's play horse and cart," said Rubella, as we pushed him out the wide opening of the garage.

"Good idea," said Antoinette. "You two hold him while I go and get the cart.

She was back in a few minutes with the cart loaded with toys.

"I thought Dohhee, and Smiler, would like a ride,"

she said, arranging her cherished toys in a small wooden box attached to two wheels and a pair of shafts. "Hold Larry still while I tie the cart on," she said, handing Rubella a bag of Guinea pig pellets.

I held onto Larry while Rubella fed him treats and Antoinette attached him to the shafts with Mum's long silk scarf.

"That should do it," she said, tying the fringed ends together.

We led him around the paddock and into the next field by bribery. The cart followed just like a real cart. It was very pleasant. Dohhee, flapped his doggy ears in the breeze and Smiler beamed with his mouth of big black stitches.

"Where's Dick?" I asked suddenly, noticing the cloth rabbit with the spotty vinyl tummy was missing.

"Oh, he is at home," said Antoinette, "I don't keep him with the others now. I hide him under my pillow."

"Why?" I asked surprised.

"His tummy glows in the dark," said Antoinette, with the air of one who reveals an important find.

"That's nothing new," I said unimpressed. "We've known that for ages."

"Yes, but I bet you didn't know I can read by its light," said Antoinette, with the smugness of a conjurer pulling flowers out of a ring-box.

"Really?"

Antoinette nodded.

"I don't believe you," said Rubella, feeding Larry

Little House in the Cow Paddock

another Guinea pig pellet.

"I can too," said Antoinette goaded into protest. "You know those Teen magazines Mum and Dad won't let me read?" We nodded.

"I read them in bed by the light of Dick's stomach!"

"I thought Mum and Dad confiscated all those magazines," I said.

"Yeah, they did, but Meagan loaned me some new ones," said Antoinette, with the swagger of a buccaneering pirate.

A natural coward myself, I gazed at my sister in admiration. "Aren't you scared of being caught?" I said, trembling with fear and delight.

"Nah," said Antoinette, "I'm not scared of Mum and Dad, any more than I am the school dental nurse."

"I think you are so brave the way you broke her picky-hook," I said admiringly, remembering the many tall tales Antoinette fabricated and I gullibly swallowed.

"You may be older than me Wendy, but you are a real goody-goody baby," said Antoinette, oozing sophisticated worldliness.

Suddenly, Mum's irate voice interrupted our fun little game. "Who took my silk scarf and tied it around that filthy sheep?"

Rubella and I looked around for Antoinette, but she had mysteriously disappeared. The only sign of our buccaneering sister, was a small dot running in the distance.

Wendy Hamilton

The Stick House in the Cow Paddock

I love work, I could watch it all day,' said the bumper sticker on the car in front of us. I could not agree more. Two weeks of school holidays at Mount Tiger lay before us; fourteen days of fabulous laziness, spiced up with the entertainment of watching others work.

"I hope I remembered everything," said Mum, as the car rose and dipped along the road.

"Don't worry," said Dad, "if you have forgotten anything you can always go back into town during the week. I'll be too busy with the subcontractors to use the car."

"I can't do that," said Mum scandalized, "that will take extra gas, petrol is getting so expensive."

"I heard on the news they are thinking of bringing in

Little House in the Cow Paddock

carless days," said Dad, changing into a lower gear as we ground up Horror Hill.

"What does that mean?" I asked, trying to get the cat who had hidden under Mum's seat.

"It means everyone has to forgo using their car one day a week to save on gas."

"Oh Harold, that will be awkward," said Mum. "We will have to choose Saturday or Sunday because you need the car to go to work."

"Meagan's family won't have to live without a car," said Antoinette, her top lip elongating and speaking in an English accent, "because they have two cars."

"They will still have to have a carless day," said Dad, "because every car has to have a bumper sticker saying which day it is not allowed on the road."

"No they won't, because they just choose a different day for each car," said Antoinette in a nasal tone (the superiority of such high social connections going to her head as usual.) "I wish we had two cars," she said, dropping back into a disgruntled New Zealand accent.

"We don't need two cars," said Mum, "two cars are a waste of money."

"This family has a god of money," said Antoinette bitterly. "When I'm grown up, I'm going to have fifteen cars and drive them whenever I want." She folded her arms and sunk down into the sheepskin seat. "And what's more," she said, sitting up quickly again as a hard piece of glue bit into her, "I'm not going to have dumb seat covers like these."

Wendy Hamilton

"There's nothing wrong with our seat covers," said Mum offended. "You girls had fun helping me stick all those sheepskin scraps on a sheet."

"Meagan's cars have sheepskins that are all the same colour and the fluff is all the same length," said Antoinette looking down her nose at our mangy multi-coloured seats.

"I'm getting very tired of hearing about all the things Meagan has," said Mum, turning around and giving Antoinette THE LOOK.

Antoinette, her head high, twisted her stiff neck and stared out the window in a black mood.

"I'm looking forward to my holidays," said Dad, changing the subject.

Mum switched off THE LOOK and turned back towards the front. "It won't be much of a holiday for you, Doggal."

"A change is as good as a holiday," said Dad, moving into a higher gear as we buzzed along a flat patch of road. "If I can get the house to the lock-up stage by the time I go back to work, I will be very happy. What are you girls going to do with your holidays?"

"We're going to have a horse show," I said, giving up on the cat, and stroking a roll of satin ribbon instead.

"Why have you only got red and blue ribbon," asked Rubella looking in the bag beside me.

"Because we have only got two horses," said Antoinette, forgetting she was in a mood. "There's no point having third place when you only have two

Little House in the Cow Paddock

horses." (The logic was watertight.) "Wendy and I are going to make heaps of rosettes and you can be the judge."

"What will you give me for judging?"

"Nothing," I said with vim. "It's an honour, you should be proud we have asked you to be the judge."

"You don't have anyone else," said Rubella, pressing her advantage. "If I don't play, you won't have a judge."

"I could give you two of my stamps," said Antoinette generously.

"Really truly? Which ones?"

"Any two you like," said Antoinette even more generously.

"Even the one from Tanzania and Queen Victoria's head?" Antoinette wavered but did not back down. "Even the one from Tanzania and Queen Victoria's head. I've got over a hundred and fifty different countries in my stamp collection now," she added proudly.

"What about you, Wendy?" said Rubella switching her attention to me. "What will you give me?"

I thought about offering her two chocolates from my secret stash, but, having only half Antoinette's generosity, cut my offer down.

"I'll give you one of my chocolates," I said in a take it or leave it tone.

"Alright, but you don't get to tell me who wins."

Antoinette and I nodded as Dad drove the car through our gateway.

"Look at all those beasts in the house," exclaimed

Wendy Hamilton

Mum angrily.

"Who left the gate open between the top field and the house paddock," said Dad, as he drove down the gravel track towards the quarry.

"Not me," we chorused.

"Mr Nobody as usual," said Dad without surprise.

"Oh, Harold, look at the mess those steers have made on my nice floor," said Mum, horrified by the mess spread liberally over the concrete. "It looks like a cowshed."

Dad parked the car by the Puriri tree and we all (including the cat) clambered out and walked over to the house site. The cattle mooed when they saw Dad coming, hoping for a new paddock.

"Get out of there," he yelled, waving his arms and shooing several fat bullocks out of our house of sticks.

"Horus lifted his tail and let out a stream of liquid pooh. It fell in a smooth brown arc, splattering in long radiating fingers as it hit the floor.

Dad frowned. "They are scouring, it will be all that spring grass," he said, looking at the vivid green pasture. He lifted up his voice, "COME ON, COME ON," he called, walking towards the gate.

The cattle kicked up their heels and scampered after him, banging heads together and scuffling about in fake fights in their excitement. When they were all where they should have been, Dad shut the gate and fastened the chain that held it shut.

"Next time, don't forget to put the chain on," he

Little House in the Cow Paddock

said, when he got back to us.

"It wasn't me," my sisters and I chorused.

Dad held up his hand, "I don't want to know who it was; I just want you to be more careful with gates."

"I can't wait until we can lock all these animals out," said Mum, turning her attention back to the house. "You kids can help unload the car and then clean all this poop off the floor while I make dinner."

"I always knew I was adopted," said Antoinette, bemoaning the loss of her royalty. "My real family would never expect me to clean up cow pooh."

"Fiddlesticks," said Mum, unmoved by Antoinette's plight, "just for that you can start cleaning pooh now while the rest of us unload the car."

"Get water from the spring," said Dad, also unperturbed, "don't use the stuff in the drums on the bench, "we don't want to run out of water before tomorrow morning."

Antoinette picked up two buckets lying nearby and stomped off to the spring, muttering dark complaints about water carrying and unnaturally cruel parents.

She was half done by the time Rubella and I joined her. As we sloshed water on the floor and swept it with stiff brooms, we talked about our horse show.

"We can make all the rosettes tomorrow morning and have the show in the afternoon," I said.

"Yeah, and that will give us time to practice a bit first," said Antoinette, scrubbing water into cow pooh. The black lump changed into an olive coloured puddle.

Wendy Hamilton

"Good idea," I nodded, sweeping dirty water out a gap in the wall and onto the grass. "We could have a go at jumping."

"We don't have any jumps," said Antoinette.

"Not yet we don't, but we can cut down a tea-tree and use a couple of rocks from the quarry to make one.

"Yeah, that will work. What other classes will we have?"

"Walking, cantering and trotting. Of course, Pretty Lady will win the trotting class."

"I'm the judge, I decide who wins," said Rubella pouting, her eyebrows going down.

"Pretty Lady always wins trotting, Dummy," I said nastily, "because Wuzzel won't trot on her sore leg."

"If you call me Dummy, I won't be the judge of your stinking show," said Rubella, stamping her foot.

"Alright, alright," I said backing down.

"Mum and Dad are mean making us do this rotten job," said Antoinette, restoring peace by waving the flag of a common enemy.

"Yeah, really mean," said Rubella, her lips sinking back into her face and her eyebrows springing back to normal.

By now the whole floor was an even olive colour.

"I suppose they will have jobs for us tomorrow morning," I said morbidly, sinking into melancholy at the thought.

We threw down the brooms and buckets and walked towards the garage.

Little House in the Cow Paddock

"Bet you a marble they won't," said Rubella, who was an optimist by nature.

"You're on," I said, as we climbed the fence and went in for dinner.

Wendy Hamilton

Preparations for the Horse Show

"You owe me a marble, Rubella," I said, holding out my hand. (We had just finished helping Dad wrap the house in pink building paper.)

Rubella peered in her marble bag and shook them around. "Here," she said, taking out a clear ball with a twist of white suspended in the middle.

"Thanks." I took it and popped it into my marble bag and pulled the drawstring shut.

"We better hurry up if we want to get the rosettes made by lunchtime," said Antoinette, lying cardboard and scissors on the table, "half the morning is gone already."

I climbed up onto my bunk, grabbed the packet sitting on the windowsill and jumped back down.

Little House in the Cow Paddock

"Did you remember to bring the stapler?" asked Antoinette.

"Of course." I opened the bag and tipped its contents onto the table; two rolls of ribbon, a stapler and a marker pen fell out. "We need a glass for the circles."

Antoinette rummaged in the wooden box where Mum kept the plates and cutlery. "Will this do?" She held up a plastic tumbler.

"Anything round will do," I nodded.

Rubella rolled marbles at the cat idly, while Antoinette and I cut cardboard circles and stapled pleated ribbon to them.

"They look a bit messy," said Antoinette looking at her blue rosette critically.

"Cover the messy bit up," I said, sticking another circle over the top of my red rosette, so that the pleats protruded neatly.

"That works," said Antoinette copying, "so long as you don't look on the back."

"Nobody is going to see the back," I said confidently, "especially if we write on the front."

Antoinette nodded, stuck the tip of her tongue out in concentration, and wrote 1st in the centre of the circle unmarred by staples. We worked away solidly and at the end of an hour we had a pile of blue and red rosettes.

"That's the last of the ribbon," I said, pulling a short length off the roll. "There is not enough left to make another one."

"Doesn't matter," said Antoinette, taking a saw

from between the jumble of gumboots by the side door, "we've got plenty. Let's go and set up a jump."

The idea seemed good to me, so we skipped in an imaginary canter down to the quarry.

"It needs to be a nice straight one," I said, as we scouted along the edge of our private dump.

"Not too fat," said Antoinette, "we don't want to spend the whole afternoon sawing."

"But not too thin either," I said, wrapping my hand around trunks systematically. "What about this one?" I shook a tree twice my height, with a trunk as thick as my wrist.

"Yeah, that one will do," said Antoinette, getting down to business with the saw. For a princess with allegedly no peasant blood, it was astonishing how slickly she dealt with that poor little tree. Within minutes it fell with a whoosh and a thud at our feet. "You get the rocks, Wend, while I cut off the branches."

"OK," I said, spotting a couple of stones as tall as my ankle. By the time I had them in line, Antoinette waded out of the bush like Daniel Boom, dragging her kill behind her. She walloped it down on the rocks.

"Looks pretty good, doesn't it?" I said admiringly.

"Yeah, just like a real jump at the A and P show," said Antoinette, wiping her hands on the seat of her trousers.

"Exactly like them," I said, imagination turning our stick and rocks into a five-bar jump, painted with stripes.

Little House in the Cow Paddock

The sound of a metal spoon banging the bottom of a pot interrupted our thoughts.

"Blow! Lunchtime, already," said Antoinette disappointed, "we will have to wait to try jumping."

"Never mind, it's better this way," I said, pretending to canter towards the shed, "we won't be interrupted when we start."

Wendy Hamilton

The Horse Show

The jumping was not going well. Wuzzel who had seen jumps before, had only three legs that worked properly. She hopped over it as if she was an old lady with a walking frame. Pretty Lady (with a full set of legs) was doing even worse.

"I don't think she has any idea about jumping," I said, as she knocked the pole off the rocks for the sixth time. "She is after all, a stock horse."

"All horses can jump, perhaps she can't see it," said Antoinette, stopping Pretty Lady directly in front of the jump. "Get her to sniff it, Wend."

I grabbed the bridle and pulled the placid horse's head down to the stick that hovered inches above the ground. She sniffed it curiously.

"Try again, now that she has seen it properly," I said.

Antoinette turned Pretty Lady around and walked a wee distance away before circling and trotting back

Little House in the Cow Paddock

towards the jump. Perhaps Antoinette was right. Perhaps Pretty Lady was shortsighted and had not seen the obstacle previously, because this time instead of ploughing right through, Pretty Lady pogoed all four legs upward, before falling to the ground like a table dropped by a crane.

"What was that?" said Antoinette, lifting her bottom up slightly. "I think my tail bone is broken."

"I don't know," I said dissolving into laughter. "That was the weirdest jump I've ever seen. It made me think of Larry when he bounces on all four feet."

"You know when I said all horses can jump," said Antoinette, sliding off Pretty Lady stiffly, "it's not true."

"I think we will have to scratch the jumping class," I said, kicking the rocks to the side and throwing the stick into the bush.

"Good idea," said Antoinette, "another jump like that and I won't be able to sit down for a week."

"Seeing as it is a show, do you think we should use my saddle?" I asked reluctantly, thinking of the gigantic monster languishing on a sawhorse. "I don't feel strong enough to carry it out of the garage."

"Forget it, Wend," said Antoinette rubbing her posterior, "I'm too sore to sit on that thing. We'll just imagine we have saddles."

"You hold the horses so they don't get their legs tangled up in the reins, and I'll go and get Rubella," I said.

Antoinette took Wuzzel's reins, and the horses

Wendy Hamilton

dropped their heads and cropped tufts of grass sprouting through the gravel. The big double door was open when I ran up the hill.

"Rubella," I hollered, "come and be the judge," meandering out. "When are you going to give me my chocolate?"

"After you judge the show," I said running inside and scooping up the pile of rosettes.

"No, I want to eat it while I watch you."

"Alright," I said giving in, "you'll have to wait until afterwards to get your stamps from Antoinette though, because she is in the quarry."

"That's all right," said Rubella, as I dumped the rosettes into her arms.

"Look the other way," I said climbing onto my bed. I waited until she turned around before pulling a small paper bag out of a hidey-hole in the rafters. I picked out a coconut chocolate because I liked them the least, before twisting the top of the bag shut, and hiding it again.

"Here you go," I said, jumping down and handing it to her. "you go and sit on the edge of the quarry and we will start the show soon."

"What am I going to sit on?" said Rubella.

"The ground."

"I can't sit on the ground," said Rubella grandly, "a judge would not sit on the damp ground." Although she was not the princess of the family, she was doing a pretty good imitation of it. All she needed was the

Little House in the Cow Paddock

English accent.

"Get me a chair if you want me to judge," she said, popping the chocolate into her mouth before I could demand it back.

"Fine, you little rat." I grabbed a campstool and marching up to the edge of the hill. I flicked it open and rammed its skinny feet into the pasture.

Rubella sat on it. "Hurry up," she mumbled through chocolate, "I don't want this to take all day."

I took a shortcut and slipped and slid down the steep quarry wall, gaining momentum as I progressed downwards. Nearing the bottom, I ran in quick tiny steps and jumped the last few feet. "You start," I said to Antoinette, giving her a boost onto Pretty Lady.

"We should have made a cardboard megaphone," said Antoinette scrambling up.

"Never mind, we will make one next time."

She nodded and gathered up the reins, while I cupped my hands around my mouth and yelled at the judge, "this is Antoinette riding Pretty Lady."

"No, no," said Antoinette interrupting me, "I'm Queen Tutankhamen riding my Arab stallion Thunderbolt."

"This is Queen Tutankhamen riding her Arab stallion Thunderbolt, in the Walking Class," I yelled officiously.

Pretty Lady minced around the perimeter of the quarry, stumbling a few times over unexpected rocks and pebbles. Then it was my turn. I took a flying leap at Wuzzel and landed stomach first over her back. I hung

Wendy Hamilton

like a sack of wheat for a few seconds before hoisting my leg over her rump and sitting up. Then I cupped my hands around my mouth again and shouted, "this is Chief Sitting Bull riding his Appaloosa, Swift Arrow, in the Walking Class."

I picked up the reins that hung limply over Wuzzel's neck and flapped my legs. "Come on Swift Arrow," I said in a deep voice. "Make Chief Sitting Bull proud." Obediently, Wuzzel tiptoed gingerly around the edge of the quarry floor, stumbling over the same rocks and pebbles as her competitor. When we were finished, we lined up next to Queen Tutankhamen and Thunderbolt, and looked at the judge expectantly.

"The winners are Queen Tutankhamen and Thunderbolt," yelled the Judge," chucking a blue rosette down into the quarry.

"That's not fair, Rubella, Wuzzel should have won," I shouted, turning back into Wendy. "The next class is trotting and Wuzzel can't trot."

"You said I could decide who won."

"Yes, but you have to be fair, Wuzzel has to win this class."

"Not if I don't want her to. I'm the judge and I can decide Queen What's-Her-Name and Lightning-Bolt can win them all if I want."

"You're a rotten judge," I shouted at her.

"And this is a rotten game," said Rubella, standing up and throwing all the rosettes and the campstool into the quarry.

Little House in the Cow Paddock

"I gave you a chocolate," I yelled

"Here you can have it back," yelled Rubella, pretending to be sick before stalking off.

"We don't need a judge anyway," said Antoinette unperturbed, "we can just take it in turns to win."

It was an inspired idea. The show went much better without a judge. Both horses performed gloriously. By the end of the afternoon their bridles bristled with equal numbers of blue and red rosettes.

"That was a jolly good show," I said to Antoinette, as I stripped the last rosette from Wuzzel's bridle and let her go.

"Yes, it was." She rubbed the seat of her pants ruefully. "I only regret trying to make Pretty Lady jump, "

"Oh, I don't regret that," I said giggling at the memory, "my only regret is giving Rubella a chocolate too soon."

Wendy Hamilton

Contractors and Wind

Music blared from a transistor radio propped on the ridge of the roof, while a team of men expertly laid tiles in long overlapping rows. Antoinette, Rubella and I (hidden in a nearby tree) lounged in the branches watching.

"This is my idea of work," said Antoinette, swinging a leg and biting into an apple.

"Yeah, me too. I love work, I could watch it all day," I said, quoting a wise bumper sticker I once saw on the back of a car.

"It must be horrible in the hot sun with all those black tiles," gloated Rubella, idly sucking a lollypop.

"Simply awful." I celebrated the fact we were in the shade by popping a chocolate in my mouth.

Little House in the Cow Paddock

We lounged on wide branches.

Wendy Hamilton

The relaxed and indolent mood in the tree tensed as our father staggered around the corner carrying a sheet of wallboard.

"I hope Dad doesn't want any help," said Antoinette, hastily pulling her leg up and out of sight.

"He's not looking for us," said Rubella optimistically.

"Not yet," I said darkly, "but he will."

After that, the apple, lollypop, and chocolate, did not taste quite so good, and the pleasure of watching work was tempered by the idea we might be hauled in to help. For once, our fears were unfounded. Dad jiggled the board expertly into place on the wall, used his hip and one hand to hold it, and nailed it home with the other. By lunchtime, the south wall of the garage was clad, and half the tiles were on the roof. But the hot sun of mid-morning had passed away and an unpleasant breeze blew.

"I'm going inside," said Antoinette, backing down the tree trunk like a possum.

"Me too," said Rubella, while I nodded.

Dad was talking to Mum when we got there. "I hope we get the roof finished before that wind gets any stronger," he said, glancing at the clouds through the window.

Mum handed Dad a pot of tea and a packet of sandwiches, "what about the building paper, could the wind rip that off?"

"Yes," said Dad with a worried frown, "but if it does, it won't cost as much as tiles to replace. At least

Little House in the Cow Paddock

it's blowing from the south, the cladding will take the brunt of it if it blows into a storm."

He picked up a cup and went off to have his lunch with the workmen.

"Why is Dad having his lunch over in the house?" said Rubella, watching him go.

"Because your father used to be a foreman, and thinks it is important to always eat with his workers."

"But they are not his workers, they are contractors," I said.

"Doesn't make any difference," said Mum, "it shows respect."

The wind whistled softly and leaves skipped across the paddock as we ate lunch and did the dishes. It was too cold to watch work now. Mum sat in bed knitting, while Antoinette and Rubella played cards and I read. All was quiet, no music blared from the ridgeline, the transistor radio sat silent in its owner's workbag. All afternoon the wind strengthened. By the time the men left it was blowing hard, and Mum had lit the lantern when Dad came in tired and hungry.

"Well, they got it done," he said in satisfaction as he unlaced his work boots. "At least the roof is all tightly buttoned up. So long as the wind doesn't change direction it won't be able to get under it and lift the tiles off."

"Is that possible?" said Mum, her eyebrows shooting up in alarm.

"Possible but not probable," Dad reassured her,

padding across the floor in his socks. "Tiles are heavy and the wind would have to get much stronger than this to lift them up." He slumped into the armchair with the wobbly leg, and stretched out wearily.

"Come and have some dinner," said Mum, dishing stew onto five plates. She put the empty pan in the sink before filling a large kettle with water and sitting it on the camp cooker. "I'm boiling some water for a nice hot shower for you."

"I don't need hot water," said Dad stoically, "My pioneering Grandfather never had hot water to wash in. Hot water makes a man soft."

"Can I have it," I piped up hopefully.

"Me too," said Rubella.

"I'm not a man and I was born for the soft life," said Antoinette, putting on her charming face.

"I'm not boiling water for all you kids," said Mum brusquely.

Antoinette's charming face was instantly replaced by her pouty face. "Why not, you get hot water every shower?".

"It would take all night," said Mum, as we pulled out chairs and sat around the table, "and you can take that look off your face Young Lady!"

"Your mother is grown up and entitled to privileges," said Dad, who did not mind if his wife was soft. "Let's thank the Lord for this food," he said, changing the subject.

"Thank you for this food, dear Lord. amen," we

Little House in the Cow Paddock

chanted in unison.

"Did you get all the cladding on the garage, Doggal?" asked Mum, loading stew onto her fork.

"Almost," said Dad, "I've only one sheet to go. I should get that done tomorrow."

The tin shed creaked as the wind prowled around seeking gaps to get in.

"Sounds like it is blowing into a real gale," said Mum looking worried. "I hope it won't wreck your holidays and ruin our plans."

"Even if it is a hurricane, it's unlikely to last two weeks," said Dad, taking a mouthful of stew.

"No, but it could put us behind schedule."

"Don't worry, we have a bit of leeway," said Dad. "Hopefully it won't get any worse."

But it did. It knocked and buffeted me as I fought my way out the garage door and around to the shower shed; cold water slopped out of the watering-can and onto my leg as I walked. Inside the makeshift building it was not much better. The wind whistled through the eaves, sprayed through nail holes and squeezed around the edges of the door. Worst of all was the floor. A freezing gale roared along the drainage ditch under the building, and squirted up through the fence battens. My skin rose in goosebumps so big I looked like a plucked chicken as I soaped speedily and doused myself with water. When I finished it was hard to put on my winceyette pyjamas, my fingers were so numb.

"Ooh that was horrible," I whimpered as I clumped

back inside and shook off Dad's big gumboots. "I'm glad that's over and done with."

I handed the empty watering-can to Antoinette. She took it reluctantly and filled it with a small amount of water. As I lay in bed, I could hear her screaming and fussing through the wall. When it was Rubella's turn, she was surprisingly quiet and very quick.

"Did you really have a shower?" asked Mum suspiciously.

Rubella opened her big brown eyes very wide, and looked Mum confidently in the eye. "Yes," she lied. Mum sniffed her and inspected her hair. Rubella was ready for the hair test. She had dipped the hem of her hair into water so it clumped into rat's tails. "I didn't wash my hair because it isn't hair washing night," she said innocently.

"Are you sure?" said Mum wavering.

"Yes, cross my heart and hope to die."

If there was any power in that well-worn saying, she should have died on the spot. But instead of dying she favoured Mum with another wide-eyed stare, and Mum crumpled.

"Alright get into bed," she said.

In the morning the wind was still blowing hard.

"Oh Harold, I don't think you should work in that gale," said Mum. "Have the day off."

"I can't," said Dad, "I need to get the garage clad before the bricklayers come. I'm surprised it hasn't started raining yet. I've only got one piece to go, and

Little House in the Cow Paddock

I'd rather put it on now than in the rain."

He put on a coat and boots and disappeared out the door. I watched him from the window as he picked up a large sheet of plywood and staggered towards the garage. Suddenly, a huge gust knocked Dad off-balance as it whooshed under the board and lifted it up. Dad, still clinging to it rose several feet off the ground and flew a few yards before dropping to the ground once more.

"Wow, Dad flew," I yelled jumping up and down in excitement.

"Where?" asked the others crowding around.

"From there to there," I said pointing out the flight path.

"Maybe we could get a big board and hang glide off the top of the quarry," said Rubella, whose optimism bordered on stupidity.

"There are no more boards and we would end up dead at the bottom of the valley if there were," I said, with pessimism bordering on cowardice.

"Meagan's father is buying a sailing yacht, and they are going to invite me to sail in the America's Cup with them," said Antoinette in an English accent. "I bet it would go fast in a wind like this."

But our mother, who was neither a pessimist, nor an optimist, or a social climber, had the best idea of all.

"Why don't you make kites?" she said putting newspaper, bamboo rods, and string on the table.

Wendy Hamilton

Budding Entrepreneurs

The kites lay broken and abandoned on the rubbish pile. They had not been successful, but it did not matter because the wind had gone and the sun shone. Once again, we basked in the bliss of ignorance. Apart from a prickly incident when we had to stuff insulation into the walls, the house progressed without our input. We lazed under trees and played tea parties with the horses. Sometimes we rode the steers for fun and enticed Larry (with Guinea pig pellets) to leap over small jumps. But by the second week we were getting rather bored.

"The house is not so fun to skate in now," said Antoinette, picking herself off the floor. "The walls get in the way."

"Don't skate in the bedroom's," I said, with wisdom gained from painful experience, "they are too small for

Little House in the Cow Paddock

anything other than spins. If you want to skate with one leg up, do it in the lounge or the garage, and don't under any circumstance shut your eyes," I added, rubbing the bruise on my forehead.

"What's that animal doing in here?" said Mum, as Larry followed Rubella inside.

"It's all right Mum," said Rubella confidently, she waved a dustpan and short-handled broom, "I'll clean up after him."

"That's all very well for number twos," said Mum unconvinced, "but what about number ones."

"Ta-da," said Rubella, pulling her hand from behind her back and waving a child's potty about, "I'm prepared for that too."

The idea was good in theory. But in practice it was almost impossible to get the timing right; for when the potty was in the right place there was nothing to catch, and when there was something to catch, the potty was not there to catch it.

"That's it," said Mum after the sixth skating accident and the tenth Larry-puddle. "Everyone, get out of here and find something constructive to do or I'm giving you all a job."

At the dreaded three-lettered word we scarpered.

"What are we going to do?" I said, sitting at the table in the shack with a notepad.

Rubella, lying on her bed, swung her legs over her head and hoisted the trunk of her body onto her elbows.

"We could play leapfrog," she said, peddling her

Wendy Hamilton

legs in the air.

"Nah, Mum said constructive," I said, chewing the end of my pencil, "she will just say we have too much energy and tell us to fill up the water drums."

This was so true nobody bothered to reply. Instead, Rubella peddled harder, while Antoinette tried to do the splits.

"We could look in the wet weather box for inspiration," said Antoinette, hovering six inches above the floor.

"Great idea," I said, pulling a cardboard box out from under Mum and Dad's bed.

"I wish we had more money," said Antoinette, finding it impossible to go any lower. "Dad's birthday is coming up and my pocket money is never enough," she added, falling forward and onto her hands.

"You know," I said thoughtfully, as I gazed at the craft supplies, "we could make things and sell them in a roadside stall."

"Like the Steven's stall?" said Rubella, forgetting to peddle.

"Yeah."

"We don't have any daffodils or pumpkins to sell," said Antoinette, looking out the window at our uncultivated land.

"No, we don't, but we could make those woollen octopuses we made at Vacation Bible School last year," I said holding up a ball of purple yarn.

"What about bean necklaces?" said Antoinette,

Little House in the Cow Paddock

picking out a roll of fishing nylon, a jar of dried beans, and several bottles of food colouring. "They are really fashionable at the moment. Meagan has a string. She wears them with her floral bellbottom pants and a halter top."

Even Rubella's interest was caught by now. She flipped up the right way and peered into the box. "I could make shell mice," she said, taking a bag of shells and a tube of glue out.

"Don't forget pet rock dogs," said Antoinette, fingering a smooth pebble.

We were hard at it by the time Mum came in. I was braiding legs, Rubella was sticking string tails on mice, and Antoinette was boiling beans in a pot of blue dye.

"My, you are busy," said Mum pleased.

"We're going to have a roadside stall," said Rubella, dotting two eyes on the pointy end of the shell with a black marker pen.

"What a good idea," said Mum encouragingly. She picked up a pipe cleaner and a wad of tulle, "you can open a packet of soap and make swans with these if you like."

We most certainly did like. By the end of the day we had two octopuses, seven mice, four stone dogs (stuck together with pink Builder's-Bog) and three soap swans with tulle tails and pipe cleaner necks. But Antoinette's necklaces were far from ready. Long strings of multi-coloured beans dangled limp and damp, from a broom suspended over two chairs.

"How long will they take to dry?" she asked anxiously.

"A few days," said Mum, "hang them out in the sun tomorrow, eventually they will dry out and harden."

"I didn't think this one out," said Antoinette disappointed.

"You can have one of my octopuses and a swan to sell," I said.

"Thanks," said Antoinette humbly.

"And you can have one of my shell mice," said Rubella.

"Isn't that lovely behaviour," said Mum beaming. "Why can't you girls be nice to each other like that all the time?"

"Because Rubella's a donkey," I said.

"Because Wendy's a stuck-up goody-goody," said Rubella.

"Because I'd rather play with Meagan," said Antoinette.

Mum sighed, the lovely moment was broken, it was back to business as usual.

Little House in the Cow Paddock

The Stall

The red gravel road that wound past our gate was not the best location for a business. Nevertheless, we were keen to give it a go. Rubella toted a beach umbrella and a bucket up the driveway while Antoinette carried a portable card table. As the eldest, I was in charge of the valuable merchandise. I carried it in a wooden crate carefully.

"Our roadside stall needs to be just outside the gate," I said, thinking of the Steven's stall.

"Why?" said Rubella, putting the bucket down. "We could put it inside the fence, people could still see it if we left the gate open."

"Because it's not a roadside stall if it is not on the side of a road," I said, flattening all opposition with logic.

After a lengthy argument we settled on a spot on the

grassy verge close to the driveway culvert.

"Stick the umbrella where it will shade the table, Rubella," said Antoinette, opening the card table and stretching out its spindly metal legs one by one.

Rubella drove the spiked end of the umbrella into the soft dirt as Antoinette flipped the table the right way up, and set a rock in the hole under one of the legs to stabilize it.

I lowered the crate to the ground gently. "I'll put the bigger things at the back," I said, taking an octopus from the box and laying it on the felt tabletop.

"Don't get my things mixed up with yours," said Antoinette, picking out a shell mouse, soap swan, and a woollen octopus. She put them on one side of the table carefully.

"It doesn't matter," said Rubella, "yours should be the last ones that sell, because you didn't make them."

"I can't help it if my bean necklaces aren't dry yet, I told you, you can have first choice when they are finished," said Antoinette in a peeved voice, "and I won't change my mind (like you) if they sell first!"

"Shut up you two," I said, arranging the swans and stone dogs artistically.

I picked two pot plants out of the bucket and put them under the table.

"Why are you putting my ferns there?" said Rubella shifting her attention to me, "people might not see them."

"You didn't wash all the dirt off the jam jars when

Little House in the Cow Paddock

you got them out of the dump," I said, tipping up a jar to prove my point. "Mum will be mad if we get the card table all dirty. If you wanted them with the rest of our things you should have cleaned them better."

"I didn't have time," said Rubella pouting, "I didn't think of them until the last minute. How much are we going to charge for them?" she asked, changing the subject.

"I don't know," I said uncertainly, "here you price them," I said to Antoinette, passing her a pen and a box of sticky circles.

"OK." Antoinette oozed the confidence of someone with a proper system for pricing. She turned the empty crate upside down and sat on it. "What do you think someone would pay for this?" she asked, holding up Rubella's shell mouse.

It was a hard question.

"Five dollars," said Rubella.

"Fifty cents," I said.

Antoinette wrote ten cents on a blank circle and stuck it on the mouse.

"I said five dollars," said Rubella annoyed.

"Nobody's going to pay five dollars for that dumb thing," said Antoinette. "Now if it was one of my bean necklaces, that's a different story, because they are fashionable."

"What about this?" she said moving on to my soap swan, "what do you think people would pay for this?"

I thought hard. The soap cost fifty cents, the tulle

cost about twenty cents and the pipe cleaner ten cents. "A dollar," I said, adding twenty cents for profit.

"Thirty cents," said Rubella, wondering why anyone would swap money for soap.

Antoinette wrote fifty cents on a circle and stuck it on my swan.

"But it costs more than that to make," I objected, "the soap alone costs fifty cents."

"Mum paid for everything so it doesn't count," said Antoinette in a haughty tone.

I knew there was something faulty with the logic, but I couldn't put my finger on what was wrong, so I let it go.

"Hurry up, there's a car coming," said Rubella, spotting a cloud of red dust in the distance.

"Tie this on the pole of the umbrella," I said, handing her a cardboard sign with the words Four Sail written on it in wobbly letters.

Rubella did as she was told. Meanwhile, I dumped the rest of the merchandise on the table hastily, as Antoinette whacked fifty-cent price tags on everything.

"Hide, hide," I shouted, cowardice rising to meet the emergency of a customer, as the car came closer and slowed down.

"Where?" shouted Rubella, looking around in panic.

"In the stockyard," said Antoinette, dumping an honesty box on the table and clambering into the nearby cattle shoot.

Rubella and I scrambled after her, and we all peeped

Little House in the Cow Paddock

out of the gaps between the rails as the car stopped, and a man and a woman got out.

"Do you think they will take the money in the honesty box?" said Rubella, in a carrying stage whisper.

"Nah, there isn't anything in there," said Antoinette.

"Let's go, there's nothing here," said the woman, "I thought they might have had flowers or vegetables for sale." They got back into the car and drove off.

"Nothing here, I like that!" I said in a huffy tone. "Why, there is heaps on the table."

"I told you they would want daffodils and pumpkins," said Antoinette.

"Shut up you two," said Rubella, "there is another car coming."

We quietened down and stared through the gaps once more. This time we had better luck because it was an elderly couple and a child.

"Grandma and Granddad, look at this," shouted the small girl running up to our table.

"What a sweet stall," said Grandma, smiling at the spelling on our sign.

"Do you like anything Annabel?" asked Granddad.

Annabel picked up one of Rubella's mice. "This is cute," she said, "can I have it?" she asked, looking at Granddad with puppy eyes.

"What do you think Grandma," said Granddad winking, "has Bella been a good girl?"

Antoinette, Rubella, and I held our breath.

"Of course she has," said Grandma.

Wendy Hamilton

"What do you think someone would pay for this?"

Little House in the Cow Paddock

We made the thumbs-up sign to each other and started breathing again.

Granddad pulled a small wallet from his back pocket and dropped something in the honesty box.

The car had barely left when we burst out of the stockyard and ran to the stall. Rubella, who was the fastest, got there first.

"Did they leave enough money?" I shouted, as she tipped something out of the honesty box.

"Twenty cents!" said Rubella jubilantly, "more than enough."

"That's ten cents for you and five cents each for me and Wendy," said Antoinette.

"That's not fair, it was my mouse," said Rubella, "I should have it all."

"Your mouse was only ten cents," said Antoinette, "so Wendy and I can have the rest."

We had a lively and heated debate, which ended in Antoinette and I getting three cents each while Rubella got four.

Sales for the rest of the day were not brisk, and the next day things were not much better. By the time the windows were installed in the house, we had sold four ferns, two bean necklaces, a stone dog, and two mice.

"I don't think I'll bother with a stall again," I said, as we packed everything up, "this is not a good location for a business."

"It wasn't a waste of time though," said Antoinette, putting bean necklaces into the crate, "it made the holidays fun."

"Yeah," said Rubella, "and best of all, now we have plenty of things to give Dad for his birthday."

Little House in the Cow Paddock

Mum's Comb and a Bold Decision

Dad had just finished installing two garage doors.

"It is going to be so good when we can lock all the animals out," said Mum, following Dad around to the front entrance as Antoinette and I rode past on Pretty Lady.

"Two more doors and you will get your wish," said Dad. The tools in his toolkit clanked as he dumped it next to a door leaning against the wall.

Pretty Lady's ears flicked at the sound but she did not shy or stop. I tightened my grip around my sister's stomach. "Quickly Noo, turn around!" I said, looking in the kitchen window, clear through the house, and out the bedroom window on the other side, "Wuzzel has turned around."

My sister pulled Pretty Lady about and we trotted

anticlockwise, carefully keeping the house between the two horses. Wuzzel, catching glimpses of her friend when opposing windows lined up, neighed in a throaty voice and quickened her speed.

"Turn, turn," I shouted, "she's catching up."

Antoinette tried, but Pretty Lady was too slow and Wuzzel caught us. I twisted around so I was facing backwards and slid over Pretty Lady's rump and onto the ground. "We could play hairdressing," I said, scratching the root of her tail. Pretty Lady lifted her neck, shut her eyes, and twitched her muzzle into a comical expression.

"Alright," said Antoinette, slipping off, "I'll go and get the grooming gear.

I walked over to Wuzzel and started braiding her tail, in what I hoped was the sort of braid I'd seen on horses at the A and P show. Antoinette took longer than I expected, I was almost finished by the time she came back, carrying a bucket loaded with brushes and hoof picks.

"What took you so long?"

"I had a bit of trouble finding everything," said Antoinette, combing Pretty Lady's bushy hair with a fragile pale-blue comb.

"That's Mum's comb," I said, both shocked and thrilled by her cheek.

"She won't notice," said Antoinette, "she's got two."

"Yes, she will, and she will kill us when she sees," I giggled, admiration rising above horror, "why don't

Little House in the Cow Paddock

you use the horse's comb?"

"That was the thing I couldn't find," said Antoinette nonchalantly, as she teased a knot out of Pretty Lady's mane.

"You could have used your own comb."

"Heck no," said Antoinette scandalized. Her lip elongated as she added, "Meagan gave it to me for my birthday and I don't want the gold glitter to rub off."

A breeze carried Mum's voice across a short expanse of grass towards us. "When can we get the bricks laid, Doggal?"

"She will catch you," I said, adrenalin shooting through my veins at the close proximity of danger.

"No, she won't," said Antoinette, combing a piece of gorse out of Pretty Lady's mane, "she's too busy talking to Dad about the house."

It seemed my buccaneering sister was right. Mum did not glance our way as she listened to Dad's answer.

"We can't go any further until we sell the house," said Dad, expertly fitting hinges onto the front door. "We don't have anywhere near the amount of money we need for the bricks. And even if we did, the shell of a house is only half the cost."

"I suppose I should be happy," said Mum, watching him chisel out flat patches, "we didn't expect to get this far before we sold the house."

"I thought it would have sold by now," nodded Dad, drilling holes and screwing the hinges in place. "Hold this," he said, lifting the door into the open-position, and jamming a wedge under it.

"The Land Agent thought it would sell quickly," said Mum, holding it upright while Dad fixed the top hinge to the doorframe, "but it has been six months so far and still nothing."

"Well, until it sells, this is as far as we can go," repeated Dad. There was a long pause while he attached the other two hinges, and Mum gazed into the distance thoughtfully.

"You know what Doggal, I'm going to have a go at selling the house myself," she said at last.

"Really?" said Dad, swinging the door back and forth experimentally. "That's a good idea. I don't know why we haven't thought of it before, you could sell sand to a Bedouin."

"I'll put a small ad in the classified column," said Mum looking pleased, as Dad trimmed a bit off the edge of the door with a hand-plane.

"There that does it," he said, shutting the door and opening it again. He twisted the key back and forth, checking that it locked properly.

"Watch out, Antoinette, hide the comb," I said, "Dad's nearly finished the door."

Antoinette dropped Mum's comb into the bucket and covered it with a coarse brush (bristling with horsehair.)

"I can't do worse than the Land Agents have," said Mum, as Dad picked up his toolkit.

"You've got nothing to lose," nodded Dad. They walked past us and around the corner of the house to

Little House in the Cow Paddock

the side entrance.

"That was close," I said, relaxing as our parent's voices faded. I picked a wildflower and poked it into Wuzzel's mane.

Antoinette, meanwhile, shifted around behind her horse. Without calves to chew it short, Pretty Lady's tail had blossomed into a glorious ornament. It cascaded from her rear end to the ground like a glossy black waterfall. While Antoinette braided Pretty Lady's tail, I picked buttercups and linked them into a fragile chain. A bumblebee buzzed past me lazily, and I could hear the steady munching of the cattle nearby. Everything was peaceful until Rubella came flying around the corner, her face red with running.

"Hurry," she shouted, "a flock of wild goats has come out of the bush. If you come now, you can see them in the back paddock."

Antoinette took Pretty Lady's bridle off hastily, while I grabbed the bucket and we ran after Rubella.

"You can see them on the other hill from the window of the garage," said Rubella, as we dumped the horse's gear in Antoinette's shed. "There are lots of little kids running around."

We followed her into the garage, clambered onto my bed, and stuck our faces close to the window. In our eagerness to see the kids, neither Antoinette nor I gave Mum's comb another thought. It languished forgotten and hidden under the hairy horse brush, like a ticking time bomb.

Wendy Hamilton

Fourteen lazy days lay before us.

Little House in the Cow Paddock

God Sells the House

For weeks the words 'House for Sale' hung in the classified column like bait on the end of a fishing rod. But Mum was not having any more luck at selling than the land agents. The fish were not biting.

"Don't you care Lord?" she cried out to heaven one day in frustration. "Please sell the house."

It was a silly question, of course he cared. That afternoon Mum got a nibble.

The phone rang.

"Hello?"

"Hello, you have a house for sale?" said a soft voice.

"Yes," gasped Mum, suddenly breathless.

"My name is Laurie Evans, and I am looking for a small low maintenance house, suitable for retirement."

"Oh dear," said Mum, her heart sinking. "Our home is a large house suitable for a family."

Wendy Hamilton

"Oh," said Laurie, there was a small pause, long enough for Mum to expect the next words to be 'thank you very much, goodbye. Instead, he said: "Is it low maintenance?"

"Well yes, it's brick and tile, but the window frames are wooden and half of them are two stories high," sighed Mum.

"Oh dear," said Laurie sadly. "Does it have a small easy-care section?"

"Not at all," said Mum (hope extinguished.) "The yard is larger than usual, there is a chicken house, a big vegetable garden, lots of trees, and a creek behind a stonewall."

"I've always wanted a stonewall," said Laurie in a wistful voice. "It has been a dream of mine since childhood."

"Really?" said Mum, hope rekindling.

"Where is the house situated?"

"On Kamo Road."

"Oh dear," the voice on the other end of the phone suddenly sounded depressed. "That is a busy road, we can't be anywhere that might endanger THE CAT."

"Oh, so you have a cat, do you?" said Mum, with a flash of inspiration as to who the real buyer was. "The cat would be perfectly safe here."

"Really?" the voice brightened.

"Yes really," Mum reassured him. "We are situated down a long right-of-way and fields border two of the boundaries. Our neighbours love cats and nobody has a

Little House in the Cow Paddock

dog. Perhaps you and your wife would like to come and look at the place. Where are you calling from?"

"Wellington," said Laurie.

"Wellington, that's six hundred miles away! Why do you want to shift all the way up here?"

"Our daughter and her family live in Whangarei."

"Oh, that's nice. Have you any grandchildren?"

"Yes, we have two granddaughters aged eight and ten."

"I forgot to say there is also a playhouse," said Mum. "Our girls used to love playing in it when they were that age. It has two little bunks and sometimes they used to spend the night in it."

"A playhouse," murmured Laurie, "in an area safe enough for children to sleep outside. That sounds like a good environment for THE CAT."

"Perhaps you and your wife would like to come and see the house?" repeated Mum.

"I could," said Laurie, stressing the I, "but my wife is sending me to buy the house because she has to stay at home to look after THE CAT."

"Of course," said Mum, speaking as if leaving a husband to buy a house unsupervised because of a cat, was the most natural thing in the world.

"I've always wanted a stonewall," said Laurie, drifting back to his childhood dream.

"The cat would love the stonewall," said Mum, "and of course the creek and small wilderness behind is a safe and healthy environment for a cat."

Wendy Hamilton

"That's right," said Laurie, taking the bait, "I think I'll drive up and see if THE CAT would like it."

Three days later, a small man got carefully out of his car.

"Hello, you must be Laurie," said Mum.

"And you must be Anne," said Laurie, shaking her hand.

"Oh dear," said Mum, as he pulled a walking stick out of the car. "I must have forgotten to tell you the house is split-level and there are two sets of stairs. I don't think this would be a good house for you."

"I know, you told me that on the phone," said Laurie. "THE CAT loves climbing stairs. The more the better."

"What about you?" asked Mum, as he tottered along the path behind her. "You might find the stairs too much."

"Oh, I'll be alright," said Laurie, brushing her concern aside. "I had a hip replacement six weeks ago, that's why I'm limping. I'll be right in a few weeks."

"So, this is the stone wall," he said, stopping beside it. He poked it with his stick. "It is lovely, I see your cat likes to sit on it," he said stroking Shnike.

"Oh yes, he often sits out here, the rocks get nice and warm. And sometimes he likes to wander about in the little wilderness on the other side of the creek."

Laurie gazed at the chicken house and large vegetable garden. "This is the perfect environment for THE CAT," he murmured, his eyes going glazy.

"Wouldn't the yard be too much for you to mow?"

Little House in the Cow Paddock

said Mum, looking worried.

"We can get a gardener."

"Right then I knew the house was sold," Mum told us later. "I knew he would buy it before he had even seen inside."

"Well, you do have your father's gift for selling," said Dad admiringly.

"There is no way I sold the house through cleverness," said Mum emphatically. "I even told Laurie it wasn't a good house for him. The whole thing was way too weird."

"Do you think he was all there?" said Dad, tapping his head.

"Oh, he was sane alright. There is nothing wrong with his brain. He is a retired university lecturer and still has all his marbles."

"Does he play marbles?" asked Rubella, pricking up her ears.

"It's only an expression, Dummy. It means he's not crazy." I said crushingly. I shot a look at Mum expecting to be told off for calling my sister Dummy. But she was too preoccupied to tell me off.

"There is only one explanation," she said. "God sold the house because I asked him for help."

"I'm sure that is true," said Dad, who had seen many prayers answered. "It has the hallmarks of God. He often does things in odd ways."

"Yeah," said Mum. "He is the one who really sold the house, and THE CAT was his agent."

Wendy Hamilton

We Shift Out to Mount Tiger

The basket Mum kept her curlers in was distinctive; it was a cross between a wastepaper basket, a birdcage, and a bicycle wheel. The shape was wastepaper basket, but the sides were birdcage, and the lid was pure bicycle wheel topped with an indestructible plastic rose. I picked it out of the trailer and started walking towards the garage of the new house.

"You can carry more than that, Wendy," said Mum tetchily, emotion leaking out of her voice.

"I don't understand Mum," I whispered to Antoinette, as I picked up a bedside clock, "she fussed about the house taking so long to sell, and now it's sold she's sad."

"Yeah," agreed Antoinette in a peeved tone, "and

Little House in the Cow Paddock

she's taking it out on us."

"I'm glad we are finally living out here," I said in a superior tone, "I'm not going to miss anything."

"Everyone, come over here and help with the piano," said Dad, turning planks into a makeshift ramp.

I put Mum's curler's basket and the clock on the lid of the piano as we gathered around it.

"On the count of three," said Dad, "I want everyone to lift this onto the planks and slide it into the garage. Are you all ready?"

"Yeah, uh-huh," we agreed unenthusiastically.

"One, two, three, lift."

Dad let out a puff of air like a weight lifter and the rest of us grunted and groaned as, with popping eyes and prominent neck sinews, we inched the piano off the trailer and into the garage.

"OK rest!" said Dad, as the tiny castors under the piano made contact with the smooth concrete floor.

We slumped against the heavy instrument, breathing hard.

"I hope THE CAT likes our house," Rubella said, sliding under the overhanging keyboard. She fiddled with the foot pedals as she added, "I wonder what he looks like?"

"He must be big," said Antoinette, "did you see the size of the cat box?"

"Yeah, it took up the whole backseat, I've never seen anything like it," I said, remembering the sloppily constructed wooden box. "It was very huckery."

Wendy Hamilton

Everyone helped to shift the piano.

Little House in the Cow Paddock

"Not everyone has your father's skill," said Mum, smiling at Dad.

"Why did it have carpet stapled on the corners?" said Rubella.

"To stop the sharp edges ripping the seats and the roof lining," said Dad.

"Laurie's wife is sweet," said Mum in a wobbly voice, "I'm glad they got there just before we left, it makes me feel better about the house, knowing such a lovely woman is getting it."

"I'm not going to miss anything," I said cockily.

"Do you think THE CAT will like your playhouse, Wendy?" asked Rubella.

All of a sudden, my stomach knotted and my legs felt shaky.

"I don't care whether he does or he doesn't," I said tetchily, emotion leaking out of my voice.

"Now everyone has had a rest," said Dad breaking up the conversation, "we need to roll the piano into the corner."

"Not the corner, Harold!" Mum was scandalized by the idea. "Pianos should never be on the outer wall of a house, it plays havoc with their tuning."

"Alright, roll it into the middle of the floor and we will stack the stuff around it," said Dad.

Rubella crawled out from under the keyboard, and we huffed and puffed as we pushed it a short distance to the centre of the room.

"That will do," said Dad. (Such lovely words.)

Wendy Hamilton

"I don't know what we would have done without this garage for our furniture," said Mum.

"We would have had to hire a storage unit," said Dad.

"That sounds expensive." Mum's Scottish blood running cold at the thought. "It has turned out well that the house took so long to sell."

"Everything works together for the good of those who love God," said Dad quoting the bible.

"What does work together for good, mean?" asked Rubella.

"Eventually, God turns everything (even bad things) into good things, Dummy," I said in an unsaintly manner.

"Don't call your sister a Dummy," admonished Mum, "it is a reasonable question."

Rubella twisted her head around and smirked at me. We waited until Mum's eye was not upon us and then we poked tongues at each other.

"We can't stand here all day talking," said Dad. "We have a trailer to unload.

"Come on girls" said Mum, leading the way back to the trailer.

Bit by bit, we ferried stuff into the garage while Dad stacked chairs and flotsam and jetsam tightly around the piano. It was going to be a juggle to get everything in.

"I'm glad we used the last six weeks to bring stuff out every weekend," said Dad frowning, "but in some ways it would have been easier to deal with everything in one hit. I think I'll have to rearrange some of this stuff." He

Little House in the Cow Paddock

pointed at the cartons of linen and nonessential furniture stacked around the walls.

"Our bed and the lounge suite can go in the shack," said Mum, "and so can the dining room table."

"Good idea," said Dad, "there's no point holding onto old junky furniture when we can use our good stuff."

By evening everything was tightly packed in the garage, and the shack had improved dramatically. I still kept my tea-tree bunk (because I liked it and it was hard to remove.) But all the other makeshift stuff was in the trailer, waiting to go to the dump. That evening we ate our dinner around a wooden table with matching chairs, and afterwards, lolled on the town-couch with legs of even length. In the soft yellow lamplight, the room oozed cosiness; the walls were cluttered with framed pictures, rugs lay on the floor in layers, and my beloved spinning wheel was squeezed into a small gap between two dressing tables. Shnike was impressed with the upgrade. He spread across one of the many cushions scattered about and purred.

"Now all we need is electricity and a hot shower," I said wistfully, "then everything would be perfect."

"It's far from perfect, but at least we don't have to carry water anymore," said Antoinette with a hint of Britain in her voice. "I wish Dad had run a pipe from the pump shed up the hill years ago."

"Yeah, it's so much better to just stick the hose in the water drum and start the pump," I agreed, tickling between the cat's hind-toes, "water-carrying was horrible."

"At least that job was only heavy, not disgusting," pouted Rubella. She pronounced her sentence with deep feeling, because it was her week for cleaning the toilet.

Although Antoinette and I were in complete agreement, we refused to dignify her remark with matching complaints, because our sister's week had only just begun, and we felt the lazy girl deserved it.

"Such a pity we can't use the fridge," said Mum, lifting a bottle of milk out of a pail of water. "As the weather gets warmer it will be harder to keep food from spoiling."

"We can switch to milk powder and dried peas," said Dad.

I pulled a face. "Yuck, when are we going to get the power on?"

"We're not sure if we are," said Mum with a worried frown, "the electricity does not come this far so we have to pay for poles and lines all the way from the Carrington's place."

"Don't forget the transformer," said Dad, "We have to pay for one of those too, and the cost to get the underground cable laid all the way down our driveway is not cheap. We may have to go with some sort of alternative energy."

Antoinette, Rubella, and I gasped. Our efficient system of eavesdropping had broken down somewhere, leaving us totally unprepared for this disaster.

Little House in the Cow Paddock

"No electricity," wailed Antoinette, "how will I curl my hair without curling tongs."

"The old-fashioned way, like I do," said Mum with vim, "use curlers."

"We haven't definitely decided to go with an alternate system," soothed Dad, "we are only exploring the possibility."

"Why?" I said, my mind still reeling.

"Because the cost of hooking onto the main grid is almost a quarter of the price of building the whole house," said Mum.

"Do you remember how I said I was not going to miss anything from the house in town," I said, turning to Antoinette.

"Yeah," said Antoinette, "I remember."

"I was wrong, I'm going to miss the shower, the toilet, and the electricity, a lot."

Antoinette nodded, "the Evan's cat is a lucky animal," she said in a heartfelt tone.

Wendy Hamilton

The Walls Go Up

Once the money from the sale of the house came through, the building progressed quickly. Mum picked out the bricks and wallpaper while Dad organised subcontractors. It was thrilling to come home every night from school and see the walls rising as men methodically moved around the house laying brick upon brick. As the walls rose, the frame of the house was covered over; and the outside was not the only place disappearing from sight. Every evening and weekend, Dad nailed sheetrock onto the internal walls. One Saturday morning he gathered us around the last visible area of studs and nogs.

"Only one more sheet to go," he said, "we have something we must do before we cover it up."

"What's happening, Doggal?" said Mum, as

Little House in the Cow Paddock

mystified as us kids.

"It's an old building custom in New Zealand to put a time capsule in the wall of a new house," said Dad.

"Why?" asked Rubella.

"So when the house is demolished, historians will have the thrill of finding it," said Dad.

"Oh here!" said Mum, "I don't like to talk about pulling down the house before we've even finished building it."

"What do we put in a time capsule?" I asked, charmed by the idea.

"A current newspaper," said Dad, waving a tightly rolled newspaper dated 1977, "and a bit of history about us. Who wants to put the newspaper in the wall?"

"Ooh, me, me, ME," shouted Rubella jumping up and down.

"And who wants to write something about us," said Dad, giving the newspaper to her. "What about you, Wendy?"

I thought of my rotten spelling and shook my head. The idea that historians of the future might view it, was guaranteed to transform my words into Pidgeon English.

"I will," said Antoinette with brazen confidence.

"Alright," said Dad, handing her a pen and notepaper.

"What shall I write?" said Antoinette, licking the end of the pen thoughtfully.

"Put down who we are," I said, full of suggestions now that I did not have to write them down.

Wendy Hamilton

"Very good," nodded Dad.

'Harold Johnson built this house in 1977 wrote Antoinette laboriously as we all stared at her. "Don't watch, it's' putting me off," she said looking up and covering her writing with her hand. Everyone (except Mum who was excellent at spelling) felt this was entirely reasonable. We turned around and watched a fly crawl over the windowpane while Antoinette's pen crawled over the paper. At length she stopped and put down the pen. "I've finished," she said, glowing with accomplishment.

"Read it out loud," said Dad encouragingly.

Antoinette puffed out her chest with importance, cleared her throat, and read, "Harold Johnson built this house in 1977. Thirteen-year-old Antoinette, eleven-year-old Rubella, and fifteen-year-old Wendy, are his children, and their mother is Anne Bell.",

"Bell!" exclaimed Mum. "Why did you give me my maiden name? Everyone will think your father and I were not married!"

"Dad said it was for the historians," said Antoinette unmoved, "so they will want to know your maiden name, besides I can't change it now because it's written in pen."

"I think you should rewrite it," said Mum.

"I forgot to put Mum's age down," said Antoinette, suddenly frowning, "perhaps I should add it."

"It will do," said Dad anxious to get back to work. (The time capsule ceremony was taking longer than he

Little House in the Cow Paddock

expected.)

"Oh, get on with it," said Mum, regretting she had not written the note herself, "I'll be dead by the time it's found."

"Rubella, put the paper in the wall," said Dad, pointing to a shelf made by a horizontal nog, "and Antoinette, put your note on top."

My sisters did as they were told, and Dad sealed up the wall with the final sheet of wallboard.

"How are we going to get into the roof to play our ukuleles now?" I said, looking at the smooth walls, "we will have to use the ladder."

"Don't bother getting the ladder," said Dad, banging the last nail home, "you won't have time, I need you all to hold up the ceiling for me, and when we are finished the only way into the roof will be by the manhole."

"What a pity," said Antoinette, "sitting up there was fun."

I thought so too, in fact, I was all for leaving the ceiling unfinished, especially once the job of finishing it got underway. But as usual nobody (meaning the parents) bothered to listen to me. Instead, Dad placed sawhorses and kitchen chairs around the room in a five-of-diamonds pattern, before marching us over to a large stack of sheetrock.

"OK, everyone…" he said.

I sighed, I was really going off that phrase. 'OK everyone' never proceeded the words 'let's have an ice cream' or 'let's be lazy for the day.'

Wendy Hamilton

"I want you to pick up this board," he continued, "then we are going to carry it through to the bedroom, and lift it up onto the roof. Got it?"

We nodded unenthusiastically before hoisting it up; staggering awkwardly down the wide hallway, and (with an upward tilt) through a bedroom door.

"We'll start in the corner by the window," puffed Dad.

Nobody said anything (because we were breathing too heavily). We scuttled in unison, like a squashed slater, across the room and into place. Dad climbed onto the sawhorse in the middle of the five-of-diamonds, while the rest of us clambered onto the chairs in the four corners.

"Lift her up," said Dad, pushing skywards, "that's right, hold it there," he said, letting go gently, "I won't be a minute."

He jumped down and moved swiftly to the side. Meanwhile, our arms shook as fire kindled in our muscles.

"What are you doing, Harold?" puffed Mum in a peeved tone, because the fire was rapidly turning into a raging furnace

"Hold on, I'll be there in a minute," said Dad, picking up what appeared to be two giant tee-squares. He ran back and jammed them (horizontal end up) between the floor and the sheetrock, one at either end. "OK, you can let go now."

Oh, the blessed relief. We dropped our arms instantly

Little House in the Cow Paddock

and rubbed our biceps. For the next few minutes we luxuriated in unskilled ignorance as Dad nailed the ceiling in place. Alas, the break was not nearly long enough, all too soon it was back to the pile, then shuffling like a slater, and more fire in the arms.

"You don't realise how big the ceiling is until you have to hold it up one sheet at a time," said Rubella, speaking a profound truth.

"This too shall pass," murmured Mum.

Everything seems longer when your arms are on fire, but eventually (as Mum foretold) all the ceiling was up.

"I'm glad that is over," I said, as we dropped our arms and climbed off our diamond for the last time.

"My real family would never have expected me to work as a labourer," said Antoinette in an English accent. "To think I could have been at the A and P show with Meagan, riding the Ferris wheel and eating candyfloss, if Mum and Dad had let me."

"Oh, we are not going through all this adopted bit again, are we?" said Mum, rubbing her arms, "just because you're put out over us saying no."

"We can't always have what we want, Antoinette," lectured Dad. "You're part of this family and we needed your help."

"Can I go to the show tomorrow?" said Antoinette. "Andrea is going tomorrow. I could go with her."

"No, I need your help tomorrow too."

Antoinette stamped her foot. "What for?"

"The sheetrock needs plastering."

"I wish I could rewrite that note I put in the wall," pouted Antoinette.

"Do you regret writing my name wrong?" said Mum touched (she was always hoping for an emotional connection with Antoinette.)

"No," said Antoinette, stamping her foot again, "I should have added, 'my parents are slave drivers!'"

Little House in the Cow Paddock

Mum's Curlers

It was the school holidays once more; the sky was a cloudless blue and skylarks warbled overhead. Long days stretched out in delicious idleness and life could not be better. I lay on my bunk with my foot lazily resting on the side of the window, as I sucked sweets and read a novel. Meanwhile, Rubella lounged on the couch and played with a puzzle. Suddenly, the peace was shattered.

"Has anyone seen my blue comb?" said Mum, coming in from the shower, her wet hair was spikey and stuck out in strange angles, "my pink comb broke."

"You can use mine," I said, offering her a coarse rake.

"I don't want one of those silly afro combs," grumbled Mum, "I don't know why you girls bother with them, you have straight hair."

"They're fashionable," I said, "and it is possible to comb hair with them.

"Well, it's not going to work for me," said Mum, "I need to set my hair."

"Why?" said Rubella, rolling a ballbearing around a miniature maze.

"Because Dad and I are going to a work-do." (Mum always called outings 'dos' unless it was a church-do; then it was a 'bunfight.')

"What work-do?" said Rubella.

"The Christmas party, Dozo," I said, "we live in one room, how did you miss that?"

"Dunno," said Rubella, rolling the ball through another gap.

I waited for Mum to rebuke me for calling my sister Dozo, but she was too busy hunting for her comb to notice. Antoinette meandered in aimlessly. Mum paused in her search when she saw her. "Do you know where my blue comb has gone, Antoinette?"

"No," said Antoinette without putting much thought into her answer.

"I'll give fifty cents to anyone who finds my comb," said Mum in desperation.

Immediately, the lazy holiday mood changed into the efficiency of a hospital emergency room. I leapt down from my bed as Rubella catapulted off the couch. Of Antoinette there was no sign; only the gently swinging door told of her speedy exit. Rubella had just thrown all

Little House in the Cow Paddock

the couch cushions on the floor, and I had merely begun searching under the beds, before she was back.

"I found it," she said, holding the comb behind her back as if she were about to give Mum a present.

"Oh, The Family's-Finder," said Mum, calling Antoinette by her pet name, "I might have known The-Family's-Finder would find it."

"Do I get fifty cents?" said Antoinette, still holding the comb behind her back.

"Of course," beamed Mum, "that was the deal."

"Here you are," said Antoinette, displaying it with the flourish of a magician pulling a rabbit out of a hat.

The comb in Antoinette's hand was grimy with brown grease. Worst of all, an abundance of horse hairs bristled from the teeth like long black strings of dental floss.

"Oh, here!" exclaimed Mum outraged. "You girls have been very naughty using my comb for the horses."

"Do I still get my fifty cents?" asked Antoinette unperturbed.

"Fifty cents! I should think not," said Mum. "You are lucky I haven't fined you fifty cents for taking my things."

"But you promised," pouted Antoinette, standing her ground.

Rubella and I in a rare moment of sisterly solidarity (and because we stood to gain a third of a bag of sweets if we won) joined forces with Antoinette.

"A promise is a promise," Rubella said, giving Mum

Wendy Hamilton

a blast of puppy-eyes.

"It's not Christian to break a promise," I said piously.

"Oh, all right," said Mum giving in, and digging fifty cents out of her purse, "here you go," she said slapping it into Antoinette's hand. "If I catch any of you kids using my things on the horses or that jolly lamb, I'm fining you, a…a…a…dollar," she stuttered, glaring at us one at a time, "and that means combs, brushes, hats, scarves, blankets, or anything else!"

The emergency atmosphere in the room, by now, had morphed into a mood of an armed truce, as Mum scrubbed her comb clean and we argued over the best way to spend Antoinette's windfall.

"Does anyone know where my curlers are?" asked Mum combing [1]Dippidy-Do through her hair.

I was about to join in the NO-chorus when a misty image of a black basket topped with a red rose, and the piano, floated into my mind. When the fog in my brain cleared, I remembered exactly where Mum's curlers were.

"They are on the piano in the garage."

"Oh no!" Mum's face was a picture of shock and horror. "That's right in the middle, I'd have to unpack the whole garage to get them." There was a pause before she asked (with a glimmer of hope in her voice) "are you sure that's where they are?"

"Absolutely sure," I nodded emphatically, "I put them there when we shifted the piano."

---
1   Hair Gel

Little House in the Cow Paddock

"Well that's that," said Mum in a tone of finality. "I'll have to think up another way to set my hair. Hmm, what would act like curlers?"

I suggested the insides of toilet rolls, but there were not enough in the rubbish-bin.

Antoinette suggested Lego blocks, but they were also packed away.

Rubella suggested carrots, which was silly, because the horses had eaten them all.

It was Mum who had the brainstorm of kindling.

"I hope Sue Carrington doesn't call around this afternoon," she said, as she twisted her hair around little sticks and secured them with bobby pins.

It is not wise to express that sort of fear in front of a pack of kids. Antoinette, Rubella, and I, exchanged sneaky smiles.

"Mrs Carrington is coming," I shouted, throwing my book down and staring through the window intently. My acting was superb; an Oscar-winning performance (even if I say so myself.) It certainly fooled my mother.

"Oh no," she said, tearing kindling out of her hair hastily.

"Heh heh, got you," I sniggered as the other's laughed.

"Mum, Mrs Carrington's coming down the driveway," said Antoinette, rushing through the door and onto centre stage. Her performance was also Oscar-winning.

Once again Mum started ripping kindling out of her

hair.

"Ha, ha, ha," we laughed. The joke was even better the second time.

Rubella won the third Oscar and after that we all won a second round of awards. By the time we were rolling out our third round of performances, the laughter was raucous. When you are young, life doesn't get much better than a lazy summer's day and a mother with kindling in her hair. We made the most of it, right up to the moment of unveiling.

"I hope this worked," said Mum, nervously pulling out a bobby-pin and unwinding a short length of hair.

We crowded around hoping for something weird to sprout from Mum's head.

"Look at that, it's holding its shape nicely," said Mum, peering into the mirror and patting the curl carefully. "I feel quite clever."

After that, it was disappointingly tame. While Mum combed her hair into waves, I went back to reading my book and Rubella went back to her puzzle. But Antoinette quietly picked up Mum's hairbrush, and went out to put Pretty Lady's tail in curlers.

Little House in the Cow Paddock

The House is Finished

The kitchen cabinets were in, and a large water tank sat on a nearby hill. A man with a digger dug a great moat around the house and a hole big enough for a swimming pool. Then a truck with a small portable crane attached to its side, dropped a septic tank into the hole. Once that was done, two men slotted clay pipes into a continuous string of drains that flowed from the house to the septic tank. It was all very entertaining. But the entertainment stopped when the moat had to be filled in.

"I thought we were done with digging," I grumbled, as we shovelled dirt over the pipes.

"Yeah," groaned Rubella. "This hole seems to be getting bigger the more we fill it."

"Building a house is all about digging," said

Wendy Hamilton

Antoinette bitterly. "I thought we were finished when the concrete was poured. How wrong I was."

"When I grow up, I'm never going to marry a builder," I said as I dug into the orange soil.

"You kids are such moaners," said Mum, "you'd moan if your pants were on fire." (She implied burning pants were a trivial problem.)

Nobody said anything about the irrational statement because we had been over that old argument many times before.

"It's only for two hours and then you're finished for the day," said Dad, under the erroneous idea that two hours was a light sentence. "The drains will be backfilled long before the summer holidays are over."

"I don't see why we couldn't get the man with the digger to push the dirt back," said Antoinette, looking at her chipped nail polish with concern.

"We need to cut costs where we can," said Dad.

"Huh, typical!" said Antoinette.

"You haven't heard why," said Mum, as if she was about to produce a surprise birthday cake from behind her back.

"Why?" asked Rubella.

"Because we have decided to bite the bullet and put the power on," said Mum looking thrilled.

"You mean, I will be able to use my curling tongs without plugging into something weird like a windmill or a generator?" said Antoinette brightening.

Little House in the Cow Paddock

"See your new room Dohhee."

Wendy Hamilton

"That's right," said Dad, "So you see, every spade full of dirt you put in the hole is helping to bring electricity.

The news, while it did not make the job any easier, was a huge boost to morale. We shovelled diligently, and (after thirty years) the two hours were up.

Denial is an odd thing, I knew the house was almost finished, but my mind refused to believe that life in the shack was drawing to a close. I was comfortable within the rhythm of lanterns, tee-tree bunks and dried food. Even the outhouse had a rustic charm. On a still night, the stars glittered in the black sky and the deep silence was punctuated with whistles from the rare Kiwi bird. When Mum brought wallpaper samples home and we chose the paper for our bedrooms, it still did not register the end was near.

"Do you like this one, this one, or this one?" She asked, her voice echoing in the empty room. Three kitchen chairs stood in a row facing the wall. As she spoke, Mum draped a long length of paper over the back of each chair and dropped the roll onto the seat. Antoinette, Rubella, and I, looked at them critically. The first pattern was oatmeal, the second was oatmeal with raisins scattered over it, the third was oatmeal with dried noodles and peas laid on top.

Rubella chose the oatmeal with raisins. I (with great daring) chose noodles and peas. But Antoinette was having none of them.

"I don't know how you can live with such boring

Little House in the Cow Paddock

walls," she said in an English accent, her face going all haughty, "I want something much more elegant."

"But Dear," said Mum (the older Antoinette got the more we tiptoed around her) a house looks better if the wallpapers are similar.

"I don't care," said Antoinette, her lip elongating and her neck going stiff. "Meagan got to choose her own wallpaper. I should be able to choose whatever I like. Besides, my room is not anywhere near the rest of the bedrooms."

This was true. Unlike the other bedrooms clustered together at the furthest end of the house, Antoinette's room opened off the front entrance.

"But Antoinette," Mum started to protest.

"YES?" The word was aggressive, and at that moment Antoinette looked like a cross between a camel and a mule.

Mum stopped mid-sentence, suddenly thinking of all the times she and Antoinette had locked horns over clothes. It struck her that the health of her new carpet hinged on her answer.

"I suppose it would not matter if that room was different," she conceded, remembering with a shudder, the many times Antoinette stomped up the stairs in a rage. "Next time I go into town, you can come with me and pick one out."

Antoinette rewarded Mum by softening her neck and shortening her top lip. She smiled, and we all breathed easier as the haughty face faded. "I'd like that," she said

Wendy Hamilton

in her native accent.

Two days later they went to town, and as Mum promised, Antoinette got to choose her wallpaper. Her choice was a bright yellow paper smothered with gaudy orange flowers. Rolled up it was a brave decision, stretched out it looked like a sunset threw up.

"Wow, I don't know how you got Mum to agree to this design," I said, as we watched a man in overalls hang the first drop.

"Oh, you just have to know how to handle the parents," said Antoinette nonchalantly with an arrogant little twist of her neck.

When nobody was looking, I pulled a camel-face in the window reflection, in the hopes that I too might 'handle the parents'. Alas, a look like my sister's haughty expression takes years to perfect. I did not think my expression would compel Mum to give me anything (other than a fine of fifty cents.)

"It's a bit glary in here," said Rubella, squinting as the interior decorator started on the third wall.

"It is a bit," said Antoinette giggling, "hang on a minute." She disappeared out the door. Rubella and I continued watching the wallpaper go up. It must have been rather uncomfortable for the poor man to have an audience of three chattering girls, but we did not think about that. As Antoinette predicted, she was back before long.

"Here you go," she said reaching into a beach bag slung over her shoulder. "Mum's sunglasses will make

Little House in the Cow Paddock

it look better," she said, handing them to us. She reached into the bag again.

"Those are not Mum's. Where did you get those?" I asked, as she pulled out an expensive pair and put them on. They sat on her face like the prominent headlights of a vintage car.

"Meagan, of course," said Antoinette, acting the part of a sophisticated woman of the world. The glasses, combined with her airy way of speaking, made her look all of seventeen. "Come out Dohhee and Smiler," she said, pulling her old toys out of her bag, "come and see your new room."

She held them out and pivoted. Dohhee's long ears waved gently and his little glass eyes stared at the walls mournfully. But Smiler beamed approval from his wide mouth of long black stitches.

"You're right, the room looks heaps better," said Rubella, pulling Mum's glasses on and off several times.

"You might need this in here," said Antoinette, passing me a tube of sunscreen.

I squeezed out a blob and rubbed it on my arms. "Do you think you could use the walls to read in the dark?"

"No, it's not luminous enough. I've got Dick's stomach for that," she said, pulling the fluffy rabbit out of her bag. She narrowed her eyes and gazed at it the wall speculatively. "It might work as a sunbed."

The idea seemed plausible. For the rest of the afternoon we tanned our arms by the glow radiating off the wallpaper. After Antoinette's room, the rest of the

Wendy Hamilton

house was tame. We lost interest and left the interior decorator in peace. Within a week he was finished. Moreover, the Electrical Company had done its job, and all the power tools worked (now that there was no longer any need for them.) Despite this, I refused to see that our days in the shack were finished. I whiled away the final day in town, and when I got home everything was over.

"It was absolutely marvellous," gushed Mum, ushering us into the new house. "The carpet layer came a day early and everything went much quicker than he expected."

"You've done well," said Dad, amazed at the transformation. Already it looked like a home.

"Antoinette and Rubella helped me," said Mum.

"We shifted in the beds and the table and chairs," said Rubella, catching Dad by the hand and dragging him through to the dining room.

"Don't forget the couch," said Antoinette, as he walked past.

"Look, Doggal," said Mum, opening a cupboard door under the sink bench. "I've put all the pots and pans in here."

"We filled the pantry," said Antoinette, sliding the hinged door in half and pushing it wide open.

"I thought we would continue making-do until Saturday," said Mum, nodding at the empty hole for the fridge.

"Good idea," said Dad, "it will take all of us to

Little House in the Cow Paddock

unpack the garage."

As they talked, I trailed behind disoriented and bleary-eyed. At last I could stand it no longer; I ran out of the house and over to the shack.

The garage looked like it had been plundered and ransacked, probably because it had been. My tee-tree bunk and a few other worthless things remained, but that was all. I threw myself onto my bed and burst into tears.

As I cried, my mind wandered over the last three years. I thought of the little tiny shack that was our first dwelling, and how we rolled it up the hill next to the new garage. I thought of the candles and lamps, and the day Wuzzel came inside. I thought fondly of the endless card games, and the hiss of the kerosene cooker. I remembered the struggle to sell the house, and the deep desire to live out here permanently. I smiled over Mum's kindling curlers, and the night Antoinette dropped her lipstick and new nighty down the dunny. I had loved it all, even the screeching possums, and the freezing cold shower…

"THE FREEZING COLD SHOWER," I said aloud, sitting up with a jolt. Now that was the one thing I definitely was NOT going to miss. I rolled up my sleeping bag rapidly and flew to my new bedroom. Whatever else it may lack, the new house had one huge redeeming quality, it had a deep bath and a scoldingly hot shower!

Wendy Hamilton

About the Author

Little House in the Cow Paddock is based on Wendy's childhood at Mount Tiger. Later in life, she and her husband, Ian, built two cottages on the land so their four children could enjoy a similar childhood. Nowadays, she lives in Australia at the edge of the bush where in addition to possums, there are kangaroos and wombats.

Little House in the Cow Paddock

Other Children's Books By Wendy Hamilton

Children's Novels
Little House in the Bush
The Britwhistles win a Prize
The Britwhistles and the Elasticizer

Children's Picture books
The Unlucky Snails
The Unlucky Snails go to France

These can be found at
www.zealauspublishing.com

www.ingramcontent.com/pod-product-compliance
Lightning Source LLC
Chambersburg PA
CBHW021111080526
44587CB00010B/474